CW01084169

THE MASCULINE IN RELATIONSHIP

THE
MASCULINE
IN RELATIONSHIP

A Modern Blueprint for
the Relational, Sexual, and Life
Leadership Your Partner Craves

GS YOUNGBLOOD

Foreword by Dr. Robert Glover,
author of *No More Mr. Nice Guy*

TABLE OF CONTENTS

FOREWORD

Prior to my writing of this foreword, GS probably had no idea that he helped save my marriage. I am going to tell you how he did this, but first I want to talk about something called "first-order change" and "second-order change."

First-order change is when we do "A" hoping we will get "B."

For example, a husband who wants his wife to shed a few pounds of baby fat might sign her up for a gym membership or enroll her in Weight Watchers without telling her first. Or a frustrated wife might buy the newest book on communication she heard about on a morning talk show and leave it on her husband's nightstand, hoping he'll read it and open up more.

Doing A to get another person to do B – first-order behavior – is what most of us do in many areas of life. Most attempts at first-order change are nothing more than thinly veiled attempts at control. In relationships, this rarely fools the other person. If they give in to the not-so-subtle manipulation, they lose themselves. To avoid this loss of self,

1

many dig their heels in and refuse to budge – even if going along might create a positive change – in order not to be controlled or manipulated.

Though most attempts at first-order change rarely work, they're still what most of us do to try to get partners, friends, colleagues, and family members to bend to our wants. When doing A doesn't produce B, we often double down and try harder.

Even if at times this form of covert contract does seem to produce some kind of positive shift, it is almost always short-lived. On top of this, because it is fundamentally unloving and manipulative, every attempt at first-order change does damage to the fabric of the relationship. If you have ever been with someone who tried to change you, you know how unloving this feels.

The healthier alternative to first-order change is called "second-order change". Here, there is no goal. You don't do A, hoping to get B. Instead, without an agenda, you consciously do something that creates some fundamental shift in the relationship's underlying dynamic (like going to marriage counseling or stopping drinking).

Then because some aspect of the relationship system has fundamentally changed (no matter how small), the relationship changes as well. This change is inherently unpredictable but also typically more profound and longer lasting. That is why second-order change is a more powerful (and loving) way to shift relationship systems than the manipulation of first-order behavior.

I hope I haven't lost you in all of this. I've just wanted to lay the groundwork for how significantly Mr. Youngblood (okay, I'll call him GS, since I count him as a close friend) helped me shift my relationship with my wife Lupita.

Here is what happened. GS and four other men (who were all in the same men's program as I) came down to my house in Puerto Vallarta in December 2018 for a weekend writers' retreat. Each had his own project he wanted to move forward. For GS, it was this book you are holding in your hands.

One evening, GS and I were relaxing in my pool when he asked me how things were going in my marriage. I had previously shared with the men in our program that I frequently over-reacted to certain things my wife did. Basically, when her anxiety kicked in, mine did too. My response at times wasn't pretty – yelling, name-calling, threatening to leave – and I didn't feel good about any of it.

There in the pool, I shared my frustration with GS that I didn't seem to be able to step out of my own anxiety reactions to my wife's projections and accusations. On top of that, none of my first-order attempts to get my wife to change were working very well either. This was when he shared with me the three core principles of Masculine leadership presented in this book:

- Respond vs. React
- Provide Structure
- Create Safety

I asked him to repeat these principles several times. I wanted to really hear them.

I then requested that he expand on the first core principle: it rang true for me and seemed to hold the potential to shift how I was interacting with my wife – which was causing her great pain and blocking her ability to relax, trust, and follow me. As GS expanded on the differences between responding and reacting (as he does in great depth in this book), I listened and let it all sink in.

That was it. I was reacting rather than responding to my wife's pain, fear, and anxiety. I knew that changing this was the key to shifting the toxic cycles into which she and I frequently pulled each other.

My wife is amazing and I love her dearly. She is as tough as nails and tender as a kitten. I know she has had many painful experiences in life, and I know trust is a challenge for her. Yet she is the most loving, open-hearted woman I have ever known, and she treats me like a king. I sincerely wanted to give my marriage every chance to survive and thrive that I could, and I wanted her to feel the depth of my love and awe.

Following that conversation with GS, I began looking at the source of my own anxiety reactions and doubled down on practices to help ground me and connect me with my Masculine core.

A few months later, I got to spend several more days with GS at a men's retreat in Mt. Shasta, California. We had the privilege of driving together from San Francisco to Northern California and spending several nights in a house shared with a few other amazing men. During this time I got to go even deeper with GS into the whole "respond vs react" thing. He shared an amazing quote from Viktor Frankl that really pulled it all together for me:

> *"Between stimulus and response there is a space. In that space is our power to choose our response. In our response lies our growth and our freedom."*

Boom. That hit it out of the park.

A significant part of this book is about that space – the space between reacting and responding. This paradigm helped me drop even further into the Masculine grounding necessary to respond rather than react to my wife's fear-based behaviors. This transformation in MY behavior fundamentally shifted the dynamics in our marriage – second-order change.

Since these discussions with GS, my marriage has indeed shifted. I have learned to respond rather than react, provide structure, and create safety with my wife. Not only has my behavior changed, so has hers. And we would both attest that we are happier, more relaxed, more playful, and are enjoying a far deeper connection. Does she still occasionally get anxious? Yes. Do I still at times react? Yes. But she is far calmer and so am I, and we both trust that we will quickly move through whatever stresses we encounter.

The core principles that have helped transform my marriage are right here in *The Masculine in Relationship*.

I get that the whole idea of Masculinity sounds kind of outdated these days. Dating back to the '70s when Gloria Steinem declared, "*A woman needs a man like a fish needs a bicycle*," to the current #MeToo movement and the meme of "Toxic Masculinity," the concept of Masculinity – and especially "Masculine leadership" – has pretty much fallen out of favor.

GS addresses these issues and painstakingly defines what true Masculinity looks like, especially what true Masculine leadership looks like. He states:

> "*Men are lost, not knowing what it really means to live from their Masculine core in a world that seems hostile to the notion.*

The Blueprint is not based on the old model of control, compulsion, and domineering. Nor is it based on the more recent "nice guy" model that produces harmless and tentative men who find that women don't respect them. Rather, the framework is based on clarity and leadership. This is not a manual for Alpha Dogs, nor a fuzzy spiritual guide. Rather, it is a clear set of principles that help you develop your Masculine leadership. And it doesn't take anything away from Feminine power."

Aah, Feminine power.

Women these days are indeed powerful. They earn more college and graduate degrees, they climb the corporate ladder more quickly than do men, and many now look around to find a man who can match their purpose, power, and energy.

Just ask any empowered woman – it's not pretty out there.

In my thirty-plus years as a "relationship expert," I have found that women typically understand what I am talking about and respond positively when I explain the principles of Masculine leadership. When I unpack the basics (as GS does so brilliantly in this book) in couples therapy, classes, and seminars, women frequently turn to their partners and say something like, *"He gets it. He understands women."*

A woman can be a CEO, brain surgeon, successful business owner, or full-time mother and still deeply desire to let go, be led, and be emotionally and sexually penetrated by a conscious, grounded man.

It is often the strongest and most liberated women who are craving a mindful man who's got a spine and balls. These women are in charge of so many things throughout the day, they typically don't want to come home and have to be in charge of their relationship and sex life as well. They want a man who can match their passion and strength – and who can lead.

As GS puts it, "*When you embody these skills, your Masculine orientation induces her to relax back into her Feminine — a state of more playfulness, adoration, and sexual openness.*"

Here is a truth I have been sharing with men for years: a woman can't follow where a man doesn't lead.

GS states it like this: "*If you think she needs to change in order for things to get better, you'll be waiting a long time. She's not going to change. Ever. At least not on her own.*"

He continues, "*This is what you most need to know: she will only change when YOU change. When you restore your Masculine core, and from that core, lead the relationship.*"

GS's model of Masculine leadership is so simply elegant. It cuts right to the heart of things and doesn't just leave you hanging. This book is filled with principles and practices to ground you into your Masculine core and show you how to lead your partner with courage, consciousness, and love.

Want your woman to change, but first-order manipulation just isn't getting it done?

It's time for a new paradigm and a new direction. As GS states, "*The old Masculine was about control; the new Masculine is about leadership.*"

Want to know how to inspire trust, lust, and devotion in your strong woman? You've come to the right place. *The Masculine in Relationship* is exactly the second-order *Blueprint* that both you and your powerful partner can buy into and use to rekindle the flames that drew you together in the first place. Only this time around, it's gonna be even hotter!

— Dr. Robert Glover
Author of *No More Mr. Nice Guy: A Proven Plan
for Getting What You Want in Love, Sex, and Life*
Puerto Vallarta, Mexico

PREFACE

This book is very personal to me because I lived through a ten-year marriage that eventually imploded. As hard as it is to admit, I had allowed myself to become emasculated. By the end, I had given up on my needs and boundaries and spent most of my time scrambling to keep the peace or withdrawing from my then-wife. Eventually, she closed her heart and body to me.

I longed to bring more of my own power and groundedness into the relationship. But, at the time, I didn't know what that would look like.

It was a painful chapter in my life, but I lived through it. And that pain was the catalyst for a long journey of discovering what it meant to be in my own Masculine power and bring leadership to my intimate relationship. Never again will I settle for a flat or toxic situation. Never again will I chronically abdicate my leadership in relationship.

My focus now is on living in a way such that my female partner believes in me, naturally opens to me sexually, and is dedicated to me. I do this by bringing relational and sexual leadership into our relationship.

This book is the best of what I've learned, observed, figured out, created, codified, and practiced in my relationships over the last two decades. It also includes what I learned from crashing and burning in a marriage. I've been there and back.

I have spent years in relationship with a strong AND feminine woman, and my ability to live from my Masculine core is part of what keeps it juicy, even after many years together and the challenges of geographic distance between us. It is never easy, but it is worth it. I seek to practice what I preach, even while I also still fall short of my own advice from time to time. But the laboratory of real relationship is a great teacher. I'm not making up theory here. I'm living it in the real world.

This work is also inspired by my studies with some of the world's foremost teachers on spirituality, authenticity, and the Masculine-Feminine dynamic: Decker Cunov, David Deida, John Wineland, and Leonard Jacobson. David is, of course, the luminary in the arena of Masculine-Feminine Polarity. But all of them taught me so much. Their influence is woven throughout my writings, and I've done my best to credit them when I cite their specific teaching points.

Through the lens of Masculine leadership, I also pull in principles from a variety of fields: meditation, tango, women's anatomy, psychology, medicine, BDSM, Authentic Relating, and martial arts.

In addition, I draw on the fifteen years that I was an executive and entrepreneur in Silicon Valley. I apply lessons learned from business leadership to the topic of Masculine leadership. Much of the high-tech industry has evolved from control-based management to leadership that inspires. The same principles apply to Masculine leadership.

This work also includes the best of what I've learned through working with my coaching clients. May they suffer less than I did and benefit from both my mistakes and my learnings.

On a continual basis, I encounter men compromising and living passively in their relationship with a strong, capable, and loving woman. These men want to live more in their Masculine core, but don't know how. They want their woman to be open to their leadership, but feel her resistance.

In their confusion, they shrink. They become pleasers. They follow rather than lead.

The women get disinterested and irritable. Relationships end. Loneliness becomes more prevalent. Self-esteem, happiness, and whole families are impacted.

This book is my attempt to help. My deep desire is that you will create a better relationship with your woman. You CAN make this happen. You CAN learn to lead your woman. You only need to master a set of learnable skills.

You will benefit. Your woman will benefit. Your kids and friends will benefit. Everything can be different. I would not say this so definitively if I had not lived through it myself.

• • •

But, there is still one more challenge you face: a world that tells you that masculinity is toxic and passe. That it is somehow a bad thing. You are left confused about how to be.

It doesn't have to be this way. Yes, there are male bad apples. And it is up to the men to be the ones to deal with these bad apples rather than leaving the women to suffer them. But here is what I believe: **Masculine leadership does NOT equal misogyny**. Misogynists expect, demand, and force. The Masculine leader invites.

Men can fully inhabit their Masculine power AND honor women. Women can be powerful and lead their lives as they see fit AND offer their Feminine energy as a gift to their man. But a fear of being ostracized as a misogynistic asshole holds some men back. This is why we have a generation of "nice guys" and women are left wondering where all the "real men" are.

I find myself reacting strongly when I see pop culture or the media painting all masculinity as toxic, or when I see men repudiating their masculinity. I react strongly when anyone proclaims that Masculine energy is something that SHOULD NOT EXIST. Bad apples are not the norm. The Masculine CAN be healthy and a powerful force for good, and in this work I present my vision of what that looks like.

Nonetheless, it is risky to write about masculinity at a time when our society is grappling with the very real history of some men's misogyny and outright sexual abuse. As a man who has a daughter, a female lover, and many dear female friends, I love that we're heading toward more equality and respect for boundaries. Yet I struggle with the ways that gender equality often negates celebration of the differences between Masculine and Feminine energies. Let's not reject the juicy tension and dance between the two. Let us hope that a world of men and women participating equally in the workforce doesn't lead to the extinction of true femininity or masculinity outside of work.

Most women I know, both meek and strong, have expressed to me their desire to be LOVED and LED by their man. This in no way negates their ability to lead their own lives, make their own choices, and provide their own leadership in the relationship. Men and women CAN still enjoy the sexy dance between the Masculine and the Feminine.

But the old manifestation of the Masculine — based on control and a *compulsive* power imbalance — clearly doesn't work anymore in a world moving toward gender equality. Nor does the increasing emasculation of men in today's world. So I am writing this book to help define a "new Masculine", which is based on leadership and clarity as manifested in a specific three-part *Masculine Blueprint* that I will present. It involves a way of being that makes others believe that you are a man that can be trusted and followed. And, in my mind, it fully honors the reality of gender equality.

And note that my references to "your woman" do not imply possessiveness or any type control dynamic. Rather, it is a term that expresses your commitment to your partner, just as if a woman were to say "that's my man". As my friend Dr. Glover likes to say "You're mine, I'm yours, and we're both free".

• • •

And while we're talking about gender, I would like to clarify that the term "Masculine" does not refer solely to men, but rather the energy of groundedness and direction. And "Feminine" does not refer solely to women, but rather the energy of responsiveness, connection, and raw emotion. Both genders manifest a mix of both energies.

I wrote this book for straight men, with the assumption that you want to be more in your Masculine, and your woman would enjoy relaxing into her Feminine. I did this to simplify my writing and pronoun references. But since I am really just describing roles and energies rather than actual gender, readers of ALL genders, gender orientations, and sexual orientations can adapt it to their own relationship. Anyone can live the *Blueprint*.

And above all, my writing assumes that your partner has given her consent for this dance of Masculine and Feminine. That she chooses of her free will to consider opening to your lead.

• • •

Finally, I want to take this opportunity to dispel two myths.

First, don't think that you need to be smarter, richer, or more handsome to have your woman adore and respect you, follow your lead, or find you attractive. How you look, how much money you earn, and what you accomplish at work don't matter nearly as much as the degree to which you live from your Masculine core. In the next chapter, you'll hear about Derek, who found this out when his wife turned to a man without looks or money. Above all else, **women want a strong, centered man to LOVE and LEAD them.** All your other assets or shortcomings rank much lower in relevance to her.

Second, the path to sustainably being in your Masculine is not through "being more of a man" or "picking up your balls and taking charge". Testosterone-fueled proclamations can feel great, but they do little to create lasting change within you. Unfortunately, too many of the resources in this domain are based on that approach. This book is different. It will introduce you to a three-part framework for developing your Masculine core. This will include specific skills, principles, and exercises. If applied with discipline, these learnings will change you at a fundamental level.

This new *Masculine Blueprint* is a model that will make others trust and follow you. It will make your woman feel loved and led, and hopefully inspire her trust in you, lust for you, and devotion to you. It is a model that ANY man can follow, so long as you are willing to put in the effort over a long period of time to build the necessary skills, habits, and embodied way of being.

I wrote this book to help men be more successful in relationship. I know first-hand the pain of a relationship ending, particularly a marriage that includes kids. If this work can save even one marriage, and even one child from the pain of being told the family is splitting, I will feel satisfied.

In that spirit, if you are impacted by this book, please share it with other men by doing a book review and sharing on social media. I'm grateful if you can help me stay focused on being a teacher rather than a marketer. And if you'd like to go deeper into this work, consider my workshops and video courses.

I wish you luck on your journey.

— GS Youngblood
San Francisco, CA
September 2019

If you enjoy this book, please download a supplemental audiobook of GS further expanding upon some of the principles presented here.

You can find it at
gsyoungblood.com/mirdownload.

CHAPTER 1

INTRODUCTION

At its core, this is a book about how Masculine power can successfully co-exist with the strong Feminine.

It lays out a model of Masculine groundedness that you can manifest in your relationship with a strong and capable woman.

Such a woman doesn't settle for mediocre. She needs you to consistently follow through on your word, have purpose in life, remain grounded in the face of her intense emotion, make her feel safe, and provide leadership in the relationship.

When that doesn't happen, she may start to drift. Things between you will start to feel flat, contentious, or even toxic. To you, she will seem to nag and criticize more, and have less interest in sex. Fighting will be more common. More and more, she'll take the lead on things, and criticize you when you don't. When she gets really angry, you'll label it as "crazy" and blame her.

But, in truth, she's just expressing the pain of you not stepping up. It is a relationship arc that is all too common.

Fighting doesn't resolve anything. Withdrawing into work or your phone makes it worse. Contorting yourself to avoid conflict just kills her respect for you.

And waiting for her to change is a road to nowhere - she never will. At least, not of her own volition.

Because these behaviors are more often than not a symptom of you not living from your grounded, Masculine core. I'll spend the majority of this book explaining why.

But when you learn to ground yourself in your natural Masculine core, something amazing happens: her behavior starts to change. The playful, accepting, sexual woman you met long ago returns. It happens without her trying, or even realizing it. And you'll find that a lot of your relationship issues will "magically" go away.

Things will be different only when YOU'RE different. This book shows you how via the *Masculine Blueprint:* Respond vs. React, Provide Structure, and Create Safety.

This framework is not based on the old model of control, compulsion, and domineering. Nor is it based on the more recent "nice guy" model that produces harmless and tentative men who find that women don't respect them. Rather, the *Blueprint* is based on clarity and leadership.

This is not a manual for Alpha Dogs, nor a fuzzy spiritual guide. Rather, it is a clear set of principles that help you develop your Masculine leadership. And it doesn't take anything away from Feminine power.

It is a *Blueprint* for inspiring your woman's trust, lust, and devotion.

DISASTER

Let's start with the story of a client of mine whose marriage had started to unravel. The painful anecdote below is from his first couples therapy session with his wife. It illustrates the worst-case scenario for a man not bringing Masculine leadership to his relationship.

> Derek didn't quite know what to expect in this first appointment. But he wanted desperately to save his marriage. So as he was introducing himself and the reason he was there, he opened up about many things that he'd previously been afraid to admit. Then it was her turn. She dropped the bombshell. She'd been having an affair with one of their friends.
>
> Her words struck him like a freight train. He remembered falling from the couch to his knees, face in his hands, a moan emanating. Derek had started to suspect that his wife and this other man had gotten emotionally close, but never would he have guessed it would go this far. He was crushed.
>
> He was a handsome, successful man. He cared for and respected his wife. The other guy was confident, but not very handsome or successful. How could she betray their marriage? And with him?? Derek later found out that despite these shortcomings, this man had a grounded and Masculine way of being.
>
> Sure, the last several years had been hard. It seemed to have started when their first child was born. Their bickering started and got progressively louder over the years. The unspoken began to settle into layers of sediment that would later prove impossible to clear.

Eventually, everything seemed to set her off, so he began to walk on pins and needles. In order to avoid trouble, he would increasingly let go of his own boundaries and needs and do whatever she wanted. And yet she still told him he was selfish. What more did she want from him? He already felt like he'd given up most of his own desires.

She became more distant. Sex was once every other month at best, until it disappeared entirely. He'd assumed it was just a natural consequence of having three young children. He felt like he spent much of his time doing whatever it took to avoid making her mad because she was so prickly most of the time. And yet he never seemed to really make her happy, no matter how hard he tried. And now, catastrophe.

Derek was a man who had lost his way. Despite his looks and financial success (which is what we men think women want most), Derek's wife lost interest in him, closed her body to him, and eventually took up with another man (who did not have either looks or money, but apparently had something far more attractive at the time).

Derek had become emasculated. Over time he oriented himself more toward trying to keep her happy and avoiding her disapproval, and less toward standing on his own two feet. Yet, instead of making things better, it drove her further away. What happened to Derek was not right. But in some ways it was inevitable.

And this dynamic that I'm describing can also reveal itself in far less dramatic circumstances. I recently met a man at an all-day event who said to me, "*I tend to stay in the background and let [my wife] tell me what to do.*" So it was no surprise that in my observations of their interactions over the day that she seemed contemptuous of him, and that there was no overt warmth between them. Little did he know how badly she suffered from his abdication of leadership.

THE DETERIORATING RELATIONSHIP

Your relationship probably hasn't gotten as bad as Derek's. But if you're reading this book, I can probably guess a few of its characteristics. You might be experiencing a general flatness. Things are "fine", but your partner doesn't seem to be as fun and adoring as when you met her. You both are going through the motions at times.

Or it could be a little more severe. Things are a bit prickly. Your woman is often irritable and criticizes you regularly. Belly laughs and hot sex are rare. You try your best to make her happy but with only moderate success. You find yourself tentative around her — in everyday life and the bedroom. You still love her, but you tell yourself "*That's just how she is*".

Or, maybe things have gotten to a state of contempt. You argue frequently, and find yourself scrambling to do whatever it takes to avoid her wrath, which usually involves suppressing your own opinions and needs and just doing whatever she tells you. This only makes it worse.

When your resentment from this hits a boiling point, you blow up and fight with her. Or retreat into work, porn, or your phone just to get a respite. Sex is non-existent.

Deep down, in the places you don't even acknowledge to yourself, you don't feel like a real man.

And you blame her for all of it.

I have bad news for you. If you think she needs to change in order for things to get better, you'll be waiting a long time. She's not going to change. Ever. At least not on her own.

If any of this sounds like your situation, then you are likely on the path to being an emasculated man. A man that abdicates his instincts, desires, and leadership in order to avoid conflict. A man that leaves his woman to deal with "her issues" on her own.

This is what you most need to know: **she will only change when YOU change**. When you restore your Masculine core, and from that core, lead the relationship. Lead the two of you out of flatness, dysfunction, and conflict and into a more connected state. **THAT** is the model of the Masculine that I present to you. **The old Masculine was about control; the new Masculine is about leadership**.

If you are able to live this model, you'll see her "magically" revert back into the woman you remember from when you first met, without her even trying to change or realizing that she is.

Of course, she may have her own personal development work to do. But stop putting your attention there. You're not responsible for that. You can't control that. And that is not what this book is about. This book is about you working on you.

THE MASCULINE BLUEPRINT

This book will not offer vague platitudes. Rather, its foundation is a three-part framework describing a well-developed Masculine core. It does not describe external behaviors to mimic, but rather the inner dynamic of true masculinity. The three elements of this framework are:

Respond vs. React: *rather than living reactively to outside stimuli, you respond choicefully to the world.*

Provide Structure: *you live as an organizing force, providing clarity and direction to minimize the level of uncertainty and decision-making burden with which your woman must deal.*

Create Safety: *you do the things necessary to make your woman feel physically, financially, and emotionally safe, which is what enables her to relax into her natural Feminine state.*

"Being Masculine" need not be an esoteric concept. Just measure your way of being against these three reasonably objective elements.

I will introduce the full framework in Chapter 5, and Chapters 8–15 will explore each element in depth. Each will offer a set of learnable skills that will help you develop these three elements within yourself.

When you embody these skills, your Masculine orientation induces her to relax back into her Feminine — a state of more playfulness, adoration, and sexual openness. And that is when the irritability, flatness, criticizing, and sexual closure will start to abate. Because of YOUR way of being, SHE will start to change. Of course, living these skills daily is not easy, but the payoff is worth it.

This book is written for you if you want to feel more in control of your life. More grounded in yourself. More successful in your intimate relationships. If you want more sex, respect, electricity, fun, and closeness with your partner, and less meaningless bickering. You will achieve these things only by LEADING the two of you out of your current pattern of relating and into the type of relationship that you crave.

You've probably experienced men who have developed their Masculine core. They exude a certain energy, have a strong presence, and seem to be in control of their lives. It may be hard to pinpoint the specifics, but there is something in the way they move, talk, interact, make eye contact, and respond. People listen when they speak. Their partners adore rather than berate them. Women and men alike are drawn to them, and follow their lead.

That is what the Masculine looks like from the outside. And an inner Masculine core is the foundation.

And yes, it certainly helps to be tall, smart, good-looking, and rich. But those traits are FAR less important than you think. **A Masculine core is based on the capacity of your nervous system to handle intensity and the mastery of a learnable set of skills**. This is an incredibly important point that you must believe in order for this book to work for you. Being blessed with looks, brains, and money makes it easier, but they are not NECESSARY. They are just superficial sources of power. A strong Masculine core is true power.

The fate of your relationship is in your hands. I encourage you to never play the victim, but rather make the moment-by-moment choice to lead. It's easy to blame. It is a lot harder to take responsibility for your situation.

It will require a lot of effort on your part to develop the foundation. Beyond just reading this book, you'll need to commit extended time to the practices that I share as well as work through any of your own issues of emotional wounding. But if you make the commitment, life can become fundamentally different for you.

THE MASCULINE IN THE NEW WORLD

I'm sure all of that sounds great. But how can you live like this in a world that tells you that Masculine energy is toxic and therefore should not exist? That gender is obsolete. How dare you have a male identity? How dare you presume that you should LEAD?

Let's take a deep breath and not get caught up in the rancor. Resistance to the Masculine is understandable. For nearly all of human history, men have dominated women. That dynamic started to change a century ago and that change has accelerated rapidly in the early twenty-first century. But there is a lot of pent-up anger to exorcize. There are a lot of behaviors and attitudes to change. And there is no patience for that process to happen slowly.

So we need not get caught up in the drama, but rather join with the change. And we need not fight back because we feel we're "losing our power". We're not losing anything. We're making space for Feminine power. It only diminishes your own power if you believe it is a ze-ro-sum game.

And therein lies the strength of the *Blueprint* I am offering you. None of the three elements involve imposing your will on anyone. You are offering your lead as an invitation. Your woman chooses whether she wants to accept it. But I am quite certain that, absent other factors, your groundedness, direction, clarity, and protection will prove an irre-sistible combination for her. The *Blueprint* shows you how to be a man she might willingly choose to follow.

The *Blueprint* is a redefinition of what we consider to be "the Mascu-line". It is a way of being that works in a world wary of men's power because it doesn't detract from women's power. It isn't based on being domineering over others, but rather by serving them powerfully through clarity, leadership, protection, and care.

WHAT'S IN THIS BOOK?

Here I will share with you how this book is organized and what it will cover.

In Chapters 2–7, we explore the dance between the Masculine and Feminine, using the work of author and teacher David Deida as context but building on top of it. The centerpiece of this section is Chapter 5, which lays out my three-part *Blueprint* for a Masculine core around which this book is organized.

In Chapters 8–10, we will explore the first element of the redefined Masculine: Respond vs. React. We start by looking at threat and anxiety, which are the cause of reactivity and the root of nearly all of your non-Masculine behaviors. This is followed by a discussion of how knowing your emotions can make you less reactive. Finally, we'll explore embodiment practices that train your nervous system to handle intensity and anxiety.

Chapters 11–13 cover the second element of the *Blueprint*: Provide Structure. We start by establishing how critical it is for you to be solidly tapped into your own desires and preferences. This serves as the foundation for a chapter on setting direction and providing structure in your relationship and life. Finally, we will do a deep dive on how to lead in the bedroom and guide your woman into her own pleasure.

We will finish with Chapters 14 and 15, which cover the third element of the *Blueprint*: Create Safety. The bulk of this section is a chapter on what I consider to be the most important material in the book: how to handle your angry and emotional woman in a way that makes her feel safe and trusting. Then we look at how being in your heart can create an unexpected level of emotional safety for your Feminine partner.

And while most books put the good stuff up front and mostly filler in the back, I actually consider Chapters 10-15 to be some of the best material. Chapter 14 is my personal favorite, but you'll need everything before that to truly appreciate and absorb it.

• • •

We'll start our journey in Chapter 2 by identifying some of the common signs — her irritability, criticism, sexual closure, etc. — that are indicators of an absence of Masculine leadership. If these look familiar to you, then you're on the right path with this book.

CHAPTER 2

BROKEN

Flat. Contentious. Toxic. Too many men's relationships have devolved into one (or more) of these states. And most usually don't know why.

In my experience, the most common cause of these states is an absence of Masculine leadership. It is not the only cause, but it is nearly always a partial or primary contributor. And for her, it creates a very challenging situation.

You may be in denial that you're stuck in one of these states. But your woman feels it. And while you've got your head in the sand, she's becoming increasingly unhappy and more difficult to be around. This is when the criticism and chaotic, baffling emotions start to become more frequent. It behooves you to start figuring out how your lack of a Masculine core is contributing to the situation. Let's start by looking at the warning signs.

THE EARLY SIGNS

There are some markers in relationship which indicate the dynamic that I've been describing. Ask yourself, does your woman increasingly seem:

- To nag and nitpick?
- To be chronically irritable?
- Less interested in sex?
- Sarcastic?
- Unappreciative of how hard you work?
- Less fun to be around?
- To increasingly tell you what to do?
- A bit boring or flat?

At the same time, do you find yourself frequently:

- Scrambling to please her?
- Holding back your truth to avoid making her mad?
- Hesitant to initiate sex?
- Preferring work, internet, or TV to spending time with her?
- Asking her for permission to spend time with your friends?
- Deferring decisions to her in the hope that it will make her happy?
- Jokingly (but passive-aggressively) referring to her as "the boss"?
- Longing for more excitement in the relationship?

At best, there may be a general flatness that you probably believe to be natural in long-term relationships. Nothing terrible, but it feels more like you are great friends rather than the lovers you were when you first got together.

At worst, things have progressed to the level of contempt from one or both of you. Derek's wife reached this point, and his marriage imploded.

And just short of that is the relationship where you find yourself willing to do whatever it takes to please your partner, to avoid her nagging, anger, or shutdown. Yet nothing seems to work, or at least not sustainably.

What is happening here? How can a caring man with the best of intentions find himself stuck in a flat or toxic relationship? While each situation varies, **a prime contributor is when the woman does not feel loved and led by you**. This happens when you fail to provide strong and caring Masculine leadership. Instead, you spend your time chasing after her trying to please her instead of leading from a place of wisdom and groundedness.

Why does a lack of Masculine leadership have such an impact? Aren't relationships supposed to be equal partnerships between two people these days? The answer is not simple. Of course, your strong and capable woman wants to be an equal. Generally, you should consult her opinion, value her wisdom, and incorporate her needs. You should respect her capabilities and treat her as an intellectual equal.

But she still wants to feel you can LEAD her.

We will spend the entire book exploring what this looks like, but here are some simple examples:

- She wants you to stay strong, even in the face of her intense emotions, especially when they're directed at you. If you are constantly defensive and afraid of these emotions, she's probably not feeling your leadership.
- She wants you to whisk her away for a night on the town, and all the details to be handled. If you are constantly asking her "*What do you want to do?*" or waiting for her to initiate plans, she's probably not feeling your leadership.

- She wants you to have your own opinions. If you have no preferences, or constantly shift them to avoid conflicting with hers, she is probably not feeling your leadership.
- She wants to feel connected to you. If you're a stone wall that doesn't share what you're feeling, she's probably not feeling your leadership.
- She wants to feel you present with her in the moment. If you're often lost in your smartphone or thoughts of work, she's probably feeling forgotten and certainly not feeling your leadership.
- She wants you to rock her in bed, and know exactly how to handle her body. If you're tentative during sex, she's probably not feeling your leadership.
- She wants you to speak your truth and not be afraid to take a stand. If you lack candor or boundaries, she's probably not feeling your leadership.
- She wants you to handle things that are hard for her. Forgive the stereotype, but if you're heading off to work and leaving her to figure out how to deal with the clogged plumbing, she's probably not feeling your leadership.

THE NECESSITY OF POLARITY

When she feels like she has to make the decisions, take the initiative, give you permission, or manage her emotions to make you feel better, **she has to go into HER Masculine**. And a woman in her Masculine, with a man who's not, almost invariably starts to get "nagging, irritable, and sexually closed" (all of the things plaguing your relationship). Or at least that's how it looks to you. In her mind, **she's just expressing the pain of you not stepping up**.

But when you lead, she can relax. More often than not, the "nagging, irritable, and sexually closed" behaviors often disappear. Not because she made a conscious choice to suppress those behaviors. Rather, because your way of being drew her into a different state.

What I'm describing here — the embodiment of your Masculine inducing her into her Feminine — is called Polarity. It is an ancient concept, one personified by Shiva and Shakti from Hindu tradition but more recently brought to life by David Deida. He says that for juicy intimacy to flourish, there has to be one person in the Masculine pole, and one in the Feminine pole. It doesn't really matter which gender is in which pole, although our chosen context here is a man who wishes to be in his Masculine and a woman who wishes to be in her Feminine. When both are in the Masculine, there is no Polarity. And if there is no Polarity, there is no juice in the relationship, and that's where your problems start.

Using Deida's perspective on Polarity as a backdrop, the goal of this book is to show you my own perspective on developing your Masculine leadership. It is the basis of my earlier assertion: **when you change, she'll start to change**.

You will be tempted to think you need to work on your relationship *together*. But if the root of your problem is actually a lack of your Masculine leadership, then it won't help. At least not yet. I advise you to STOP trying to work it out with her, and START working on yourself. Until then, I believe it is all wasted energy. But if you put in the time to develop this part of you, I guarantee things will be different when you re-engage with her. **That's the thing about being in your Masculine — it tends to cause a lot of relationship problems to organically disappear.**

The more you lead, the more she knows you have things handled and she can relax. The more she feels safe. And the more she trusts you. It is from this place that she opens her heart and body to you. It is from this place where you get her smile and playfulness; where you get her respect, support, and adoration. This is what all men want from their woman — her trust, lust, and devotion.

I cannot emphasize enough how important trust and safety are to a woman softening and opening to you. Without them, nothing you do will ever be right. Your relationship will be perpetually dissatisfying to both of you. But the good news is that when you respond rather than react, provide structure, and create safety, the trust usually organically follows.

And guess what? If you're *not* fulfilling this role, she will be fantasizing about a man who can. Yes, that's right — your sweet little flower could be dreaming of another man who can lead her, even if it is only a man in her imagination. And **in this unfulfilled longing are born the behaviors we talked about earlier — nagging, irritability, lack of interest in sex, lack of gratitude, etc**. Rarely is the issue she complains about the actual issue — it is usually tied to a larger lack of safety and trust (we'll discuss this more in Chapter 14). In so many cases, it is rooted in a lack of Polarity brought about by your lack of a Masculine core.

A chronic lack of Polarity will be painful for you. It can leave you feeling like you're not "man enough" to lead, or at least that your woman thinks this. But, ironically, the opposite is true. The fact that she's nagging you is evidence that she knows you ARE man enough deep down. She knows you are better than this and is simply expressing her deep longing (albeit rather clumsily) for you to step up into your full potential. It is an indicator that she's still "in". **The day she stops calling**

you out is the day that she's given up on you. So begin to look more deeply into the nagging to find where an underlying kernel of truth shows you where you can grow.

• • •

There is one absolutely foundational point you must remember about conflict with your woman: **whether or not you are the problem in this dynamic, you ARE the solution.** Your Masculine leadership is the solution. It doesn't matter who or what was the cause of the latest flare-up. You need to take responsibility for the resolution.

If you don't like how your woman is being, LEAD her into a different state. Don't blame her for how things are and wait for her to change. If she's throwing wild emotion at you, LEAD her out of emotional chaos by being grounded and holding space for her intensity. If she isn't feeling sexual often enough for you, LEAD her into her sexuality by opening her heart and then knowing how to open her body. If you feel like she's mistreating you, LEAD her into respecting your boundaries by actually setting and holding those boundaries.

The result? More sex. More excitement. More attraction. Less bickering. Less rejection. A happier man. A happier woman. Relationships and families that stay intact.

Of course, you may find yourself in relationship with a woman who is chronically neurotic and caught up in her stories, wounds, and projections onto you. It may feel like no amount of your leadership will improve the situation. In such cases, it may be appropriate to exit a conversation or the relationship itself. But only AFTER you have gone down the path of bringing your full Masculine leadership to the situation.

CONCLUSION

Flatness, contention, or toxicity are not the inevitable outcomes of a long-term relationship. More often than not, they are caused by a lack of leadership and Polarity in the relationship. You contribute to this dynamic when you abdicate the Masculine role.

Unfortunately, you and all men are up against a tailwind here: our increasingly gender-neutral society tells you that masculinity is bad and that the genders are the same. Let's take a look at that dynamic in the next chapter.

CHAPTER 3

EQUALITY

It is obvious that our world has become increasingly gender-neutral, particularly in the professional realm. We're moving toward erasing gender pay gaps and sexual harassment from the workplace. The old norms of the man being the breadwinner, and the woman being financially beholden, have faded. I'm thrilled for my daughter that she'll enter a working world where the old mainstream biases are on the wane.

Many men have also changed their focus. We've gotten more in touch with our feelings and more involved in child-rearing than earlier generations of males.

There is a huge upside to this dynamic. The economy is stronger from so many talented women in the workforce. Families are able to earn more income. And kids get to spend time with both mother and father.

Give credit to the women. They stood up and said, "*This is not right.*" It has taken many years, but the payoff for them is happening.

And give credit to the men. After years of resisting, we're starting to acknowledge both our own emotions and women's sovereignty over their bodies and career opportunities.

And yet there's a massive dark side to the whole thing.

THE BIRTH OF SAMENESS

Somewhere along the way, the drive for gender equality started to slide into gender sameness. At work, the impact was positive. It created more professional opportunities for women. But in our personal and intimate domains, it began to erode our appreciation of the differences between Masculine and Feminine energies.

I can't pretend to speak for women, but many that I know say they enjoy a man in his Masculine power, one who feels grounded and decisive as long as it is coupled with caring. The Feminine nervous system relaxes in the presence of such a man. And from that relaxed place may come her smile, her playfulness, her choice to open to his capable lead, her choice to open her body to him. For them, a passive or neutral man won't evoke this response over the long term.

But popular and social media bombard men with the message that masculinity is analogous to the misogyny that has created so much pain in the world. Most men are not misogynists, but the behavior of the bad apples reflects on all men. And it creates overt hostility to the mere notion of the Masculine. Some say it should not exist, that we are all the same and any notion of the Masculine should be eradicated. Some mistakenly equate all Masculine to toxic masculinity.

So it is no surprise that many men are scared to assert themselves for fear of being shamed and ostracized. To openly proclaim that you intend to inhabit a Masculine role is risky these days.

Other men simply don't know how to be Masculine because they never had a role model for it. Popular television seems to feature mostly neutralized men, and most fathers don't explicitly teach their sons about Masculine leadership.

Women have a challenge of their own. They fought for and gained equality. But in their private intimate lives, many women still crave some degree of Masculine leadership from their man. This can feel like a paradox, one that they cannot reconcile with their strong, independent side. Both sides are real, yet they feel mutually exclusive. In an April 2012 Newsweek article, Katie Roiphe wrote:

> *"Feminists have long been perplexed by our continuing investment in this fantasy, the residual desire to be controlled or dominated in the romantic sphere. They are on the record as appalled at how many strong, successful, independent women are caught up in elaborate fantasies of submission ... "*

How can women reconcile the two? They want to be powerful and self-sufficient, and yet some occasionally find themselves dying inside for their man to just step up, "be a man", and take charge for a bit.

The truth is that strong women CAN take care of themselves. They CAN make decisions for themselves and/or their family They CAN make things happen in this world. But many just don't want to HAVE to do it all the time. My ex-wife said that to me fifteen years ago, and only now do I understand what she meant. My tendency in those days was to presume that, because she was a capable woman, I could leave her on her own to handle a lot of things. Because I was busy at work, I left the vacation planning to her. I made her call the plumber. She did all of our taxes. And I abdicated the social calendar to her as well. Of course, I was working full time and she wasn't, so she had the time for all of this. But she felt left alone to deal with these things, and it had a huge negative impact on us. She deeply felt my lack of leadership of the family.

ONE'S 'NATURAL' ENERGY

Women in a situation like this (and in the working world) are forced into their own Masculine energy. And while they have every right to be in their Masculine and get things done in the world as they choose, in many cases it is not their <u>natural</u> state. They can live in that mode for a while, but many **occasionally crave to return to and rest in their natural state of Feminine energy**, even if only temporarily. So if your woman spends too long in her Masculine energy, you may start to experience her as irritable, bossy, critical, and uninterested in sex.

It is not simply because she needs a rest from her labors. Everybody needs that. Rather, this is about her getting time in her natural Feminine state. As a man, you don't have the problem I describe above because your natural state is the Masculine, and thus you exist mostly in your natural state all day long at work. You may get tired, but it doesn't feel unnatural.

Many women are craving a man that can lead them back into that natural Feminine state. They'll tell you it's not very complicated — just do three things. First, stay strong in the face of her powerful emotions. Second, step up and take charge once in a while. And third, make her feel safe.

In fact, this is what the *Blueprint* is about. It is your path out of the tentativeness that men who are with strong women often experience. It feels good to both of you when she spends time in her Feminine rather than the two of you constantly existing in that gray fog of sameness.

That sameness is killing the spark in so many modern couples. They have become great partners or great co-parents. But passion between them — the sexuality, the playfulness, the desire — is flat. The fact is, **in our modern sophistication of equality, we can at times be bored with one another**. So we men look outside our intimate relationship for something, anything, to light us up — porn, alcohol, staring at our phones, or even infidelity.

FROM FLAT TO TOXIC

Losing Polarity can sometimes devolve into contempt. Way back in my married days I can remember being on the receiving end of my then-wife's venom. When I would make a mistake, she would amplify it into a character flaw and made damn sure I knew it.

I frequently see this out in the world. Recently at a restaurant, I overheard a couple in the lobby waiting for a table. The woman was excoriating the man for having left some item for the baby at home. At first, he tried to impotently defend himself by saying that he'd thought she'd brought it. Yet she still laid into him, "*You always leave me to think of everything ... idiot!*" Then he just gave up, sagged his shoulders, and collapsed into silence and withdrawal. Connection, attraction, generosity, openness — all gone. She trusted him to handle something and he didn't deliver. So she has to go into her Masculine to makes sure things get done. She's certainly not trusting his lead after that. But the truth is that the level of contempt she displayed was the result of a long history of him losing her trust.

This type of contempt often arises in chronically de-polarized relationships. **Her anger wasn't about the forgotten baby item**, per se. It was about her not experiencing his presence, leadership, or care for her. It was about a pattern of her feeling abandoned and forced to provide all the thinking and leadership around caring for the kids.

How could he have broken that pattern in this scenario? He could have provided structure by stopping her before they left the house and doing a final check to make sure they had everything — evidence of him being present enough to be tracking what's important. Or, when she was expressing her anger at him, he could have responded rather than reacted by holding space for her anger, and saying something like *"You know what Baby, you're right. I'm sorry I forgot it. I can see how that makes you feel you have to do this alone."* If he had done either of those two things, things might have been much different. Instead, he allowed the mood in the moment to be ruined as well as another layer to be laid down in the chronic sediment that had been forming between them.

You can see examples of this dynamic everywhere. Look around and count the number of married men you know that seem emasculated. Husbands who refer to their wives as "the boss", not out of respect but with tongue in cheek and a trace of bitterness at their own disempowerment (to which they'd never admit). You'd think that the wives love being in the driver's seat, but just the opposite is true: most of them hate it. Most women are craving for their man to be in his own power, as long as he is inclusive, collaborative, and not domineering.

Ask both men and women in these depolarized, flat, or contemptuous relationships what they think is going on and you'll hear conflicting stories. A lot of women will tell you that men have become too tentative — don't have their own opinions, don't make decisions, don't initiate, and don't lead. They've become pleasers. The women may consider them good men, but don't feel them fully grounded in their personal power. The men will tell you that females have become so assertive and demanding that they can't relax around these women, and certainly can't seem to do anything right in their eyes. On both sides, despite great intent, attraction wanes. As David Deida says:

> *"The love may still be strong, the friendship may still be strong, but the sexual polarity fades, unless in moments of intimacy one partner is willing to play the masculine pole and one partner is willing to play the feminine pole."*

Men are confused. You try to be the safe nice guy that you think women want (you've heard women exclaim *"Why can't I just meet a nice guy?"*). You try to be democratic and respectful of your woman's needs. You think pleasing her is the path to her happiness. The women love it for a while because things seem so easy with you, right up until the point they realize they are bored out of their minds by it.

Yes, she may respect your integrity, accomplishments, and the way you cater to her needs. But if she doesn't feel your Masculine leadership, the Polarity will wither, along with her desire for you.

Too many men have abdicated the "frame" of the relationship — the decision making around how you spend your time, how you spend your money, with whom you associate, how the kids are raised, etc. Men end up seeking their woman's permission for even the simplest thing that they would have done without a thought when they were single. It's *"Honey, can I go to the gym after work tonight?"* rather than that man establishing upfront in the relationship *"Honey, staying in shape is essential for me. I will be going to the gym after work at least twice a week, and I'm willing to work with you on how we can ease any burden that creates for you.*" But as Rollo Tomassi writes in his book *The Rational Male*:

> "… *frame, like power, abhors a vacuum. In the absence of the frame security a woman naturally seeks from a masculine male, this security need forces her to provide that security for herself.*"

In other words, if you don't provide frame for the relationship, she will.

These examples of abdicating the frame may look familiar:

- You offering no input into vacation planning, leaving her to decide what you two or the family will do this summer.
- You backing down when she expresses disagreement with your opinion.
- You deferring to her on how to discipline one of the children for a transgression.
- Her handling the entire social calendar, including what you do and with whom you spend time as a couple.
- Her asking for advice on how to handle a tricky interpersonal situation at work and you responding with "*Just do what you think is right.*"
- Her determining which critical house maintenance projects need to be done.
- You getting defensive over her emotional outburst rather than standing strong and leading her back into her heart.

The more you are passive in situations like these, the more she needs to go into her own Masculine and find her own solution. Is she capable of leading her own life? Yes. Will you tell yourself that you have enough to worry about and that she's a big girl and can handle her own issues?

Probably. Will this lead to the juicy, open, playful partner you're craving? Absolutely 100 percent not.

CONCLUSION

You face a headwind to inhabiting the Masculine role in today's world. A history of men's domineering and women's pain have created resistance, and in some cases, hostility to this. And in today's increasingly gender-neutral world, many men wonder if there is still a place for the Masculine.

I contend that Masculine leadership and gender equality can co-exist. This is not a zero-sum game. I do not advocate a return to past days of gender inequity. But I do stand for men manifesting more of their Masculine energy and providing more leadership in relationship. The *Blueprint* is a model for you doing that. And the more you lead well, the more it will induce her into that Feminine state. And that act of "induction" is exactly what we'll explore in the next chapter.

CHAPTER 4

INDUCTION

I hope that I have made the case that Polarity is good. But those of you who are with intelligent, independent, and strong-willed women (or women that have gotten to the point of being critical, irritable, and sexually closed) are wondering: "*How am I ever going to get her to relax into her Feminine state? That seems impossible these days.*" The answer I gave before still holds true: when you start living from your Masculine core, your way of being will naturally <u>induce</u> her to relax into her Feminine. Her way of being is strongly influenced by your own. And, yes, this even applies to strong-willed women.

You cannot demand that she go into that state, nor shame her into it. And she can't force <u>herself</u> into that state. She will only be different when YOU'RE different.

WHAT SHE WANTS

She very much wants you to just **step up and take charge once in a while**. She doesn't want to feel controlled by you or be financially dependent on you. But she does occasionally want to relax into your Masculine direction. The mainstream success of the book *50 Shades of*

Grey is evidence of this. It was not specifically the extremes of BDSM that made it so popular. Rather, it was the energy of direction, structure, and surrender that so many women found enticing.

She very much wants you to **stay strong in the face of her powerful emotions and lead her back into her Feminine heartspace**. We'll get more into this later, but it is the opposite of responding to her emotions with defensiveness, cluelessness, or withdrawal.

And she's dying for you to **be your own man**. To stand independently in your own power, not dependent on her approval or input. To have your own opinions and boundaries.

It is these qualities in you that induce her to relax. When you lead like this, she's more likely to soften into that sweet, playful, open state that you so enjoy.

This is a very important point, albeit a counterintuitive one. When your partner is irritable, critical, and sexually closed, most men just assume "*That's the way she is.*" You wait it out, hoping for it to pass. Little do you realize that you can actively change her state. And **you'll find yourself with more fun, adoration, and sex than you thought was possible in your relationship**.

LEADERSHIP IS HARD

But, make no mistake: Taking the lead is far easier said than done. There's no natural anointed position for you as the leader. In many domains, she's just as capable as you are. So you can't just stride in like a cowboy and think you're "in charge". You have to earn it over time through consistent consciousness, competence, and proactivity.

Now, for a man with a very competent woman, this can sometimes be difficult. She's so good at certain things, and probably obsesses over them far more than you do. She may often seem to be one step ahead. You find yourself having to follow HER lead as a result. One of my clients shared with me a story about this very dynamic:

> *Nate complained that his woman was obsessive about the logistics of their life. She was always thinking about what was coming next, and by the time he tuned in, she'd already worked out her own very strong opinion about how they should handle it. And she was smart, so her plans were usually pretty good. As a result, Nate always felt like he was chasing behind her, and their Polarity was suffering as a result. And he admitted that he sometimes pushed back on her ideas simply because he was feeling shame around this dynamic. He felt like she was calling all the shots and that she thought less of him for it.*

I shared two thoughts with Nate. The first was that when he resists out of ego, he only proves his weakness to his woman. The Feminine will feel his ego-driven defenses loud and clear, even though he thinks he's hiding them. I encouraged Nate to actually celebrate her competencies, welcome them, and to find ways to add structure to them. Fighting what was obvious (that she was good at thinking ahead in certain domains) was folly. In my own life, I try to make space for my woman's strengths. I know that I'm hopeless in the kitchen, and so when my woman and I cook together, I will say *"Baby, tell me what to do!"* and she'll hand me some vegetables to chop. It's a very effective technique for dealing with a situation when your woman is better suited to take the lead. You're showing leadership and adding structure, even in the context of guiding her to set some direction. This is in contrast to you trying to take charge yourself despite having less knowledge in the domain at hand, or sitting back meekly not doing anything.

The second thought I shared with Nate was that the situation could be an indicator that he was not showing up fully present. Yes, maybe his partner's mind works faster than his. But it was possible that his attention would drift a little too much to past and future rather than being in the present moment of what's happening (even though the plans were being made for the future, the time to think through them was NOW in the present). While she's naturally thinking through an upcoming situation and mapping out options, his mind would be elsewhere. In other words, maybe this was more about his lack of focus and attention than it was about her obsessiveness. I encouraged him to feel into this and see what was true. It was possible he needed to tighten up on his presence. To get more "here", now.

Although these situations were painful for Nate, they may have been a gift that illuminated for him where he needed to evolve. And my point in sharing this is that **if you're with a strong woman, you'll need to learn to incorporate her strengths into your leadership, not resist or suppress them**.

SHE WILL RESIST YOUR LEADERSHIP

But don't expect reciprocity. Your strong woman will resist you leading her. This is almost assured to happen when she's not feeling connected to you. She won't feel safe enough to surrender into your lead. I have a memory of a time I met my woman in Amsterdam after having not seen her for six weeks, and she called me from the taxi on her way to our downtown hotel. I playfully tried a little verbal dominance: "*When you get to the hotel, put on that little black dress and meet me at the wine bar down the street in exactly one hour.*" Now, I've used that line and that energy on her in other situations, and she loved it. But in this case, she was not feeling connected to me since we hadn't seen each other in a long while. So she got upset with me. My attempt at creating a little juice and Polarity fell flat because I hadn't been skillful enough to wait for the two of us to re-establish connection first.

Your woman may also resist your leadership if she's swimming in her own Masculine energy at the moment, such as when she returns home from work.

Or, she may resist simply because you've chronically abdicated the lead, and she has learned to simply rely on her own Masculine direction in the absence of yours.

In all three cases, your attempts at leading (which will feel new to her) will unfortunately be perceived as domineering, annoying, and unwelcome.

If, for whatever reason, you feel her resistance, don't foolishly try a "frontal assault" to get her to follow you. Be smarter about it and lead her back into a more relaxed state. If she's in her Masculine because of work, get her out of her head and back into her body with a foot rub, cooking her a delicious meal, or taking her outside for a walk. If the two of you aren't feeling connected, get connected with some mutual eye gazing or breathing or kissing. If she's upset about something, address it head-on with her and clear it. When you do this, you bring her into a state in which she's more likely to accept your leadership. **Take the time and definitive steps to consciously transition her out of her current state** and into one where Polarity is possible.

CONCLUSION

Too many men are passively hoping for their women to be more relaxed, flexible, forgiving, playful, sexual, and adoring. But as they say: hope is not a strategy. Your woman is that way for a reason. Too many years of you (and other men in past relationships) ignoring her pain and her needs. Difficult women are often the way they are as a defense mechanism to the unwitting "neglect" that the men in their intimate life have put them through. But as you'll see me write elsewhere in this book — **you may or may not be the problem, but you ARE the solution**. If you don't like how she is being, LEAD her into a different state.

And the first step on this journey starts with you developing your own solid Masculine core. This is what we will explore in the next chapter, with the centerpiece being the three-part *Blueprint* that describes a clear, replicable definition of what it means to be in your Masculine.

CHAPTER 5

THE MASCULINE BLUEPRINT

In 1964, Supreme Court Justice Potter Stewart tried and failed to objectively define pornography. In his opinion on *Jacobellis v. Ohio*, he wrote: *"I know it when I see it."*, and that further analysis was difficult. There are some things that are so subjective that they are difficult to objectively define.

For many men, masculinity can be the same way. They know it when they see it, but have a hard time defining it such that they could consciously replicate it within themselves. But that is exactly what we'll do in this chapter: **define an objective framework to describe the Masculine core.**

WHAT DOES MASCULINE LOOK LIKE?

Let's follow Justice Potter's lead and see what our eyes tell us. Most of us can actually spot Masculine energy very easily. There is a certain deliberateness and assuredness about a man who exudes it. You might observe that he:

- Takes charge
- Speaks confidently
- Moves deliberately
- Has strong presence
- Stands with a grounded, natural posture
- Seems unswayed by others
- Has clear boundaries
- Does not seem afraid of women's emotions
- States what he wants
- Holds a steady gaze
- Steps up to lead in a group
- Speaks his truth
- Has a strong purpose in life
- Acknowledges his emotions
- Seems fearless
- Leads his woman in sexuality
- Attracts others to him
- Is listened to when he speaks

A man who doesn't seem to be grounded in a Masculine core might:

- Be overly expressive
- Get defensive when verbally attacked
- Collapse around Feminine energy or strong Masculine energy
- Withdraw when feeling hurt
- Nervously fidget or tap his hands or feet
- Gets unconsciously angry when being shamed
- Talk too much to fill awkward silences
- Try to initiate sex indirectly rather than directly
- Compulsively try to please others
- Get nervous with a beautiful woman

- Slouch while standing or sitting
- Withdraw in the face of his woman's anger
- Move and speak rapidly
- Offer non-sequiturs in conversation
- Be lazy or lack purpose
- Deny that he's feeling angry or scared
- Be afraid to approach others in social situations
- Fail to express or hold boundaries
- Be physically out of shape
- Be unable to make a decision
- Be afraid to speak his truth
- Be ignored by others
- Have poor eye contact

Of course, we all wish the first list described us. But, inevitably, we sometimes exhibit behaviors from the second. For instance, of course you understand that you *should* speak confidently, and probably do when circumstances are easy. But sometimes you don't when the pressure is on. Not always when your woman is shouting at you. Not always when another man is challenging you at work or in the streets. And usually not when you're feeling shame or anxiety. Because **it is under these conditions of stress and threat where you tend to regress and reveal the places in which you are underdeveloped**.

Of course, you could just mimic the behaviors on the first list. But when the pressure is really on, those underdeveloped places in you will show. Others will see right through you, *especially* the women in your life because they are so perceptive. **You should never try to "act Masculine"**. Those around you will see right through it, even when you think they can't. You will come off as a poser.

That is, in fact, the shortcoming I see in most of the popular advice out there about masculinity — the authors essentially shout at you to "*BE MORE CONFIDENT!*" as they try to coach you into becoming an Alpha Male. But they don't tell you HOW exactly to go about doing it, so all you can do is fake it. You're left confused as to what it takes to be genuinely in your Masculine.

And in this, the truth of things is revealed: **you cannot fake masculinity nor will you become more Masculine by copying behaviors**. Instead, it is your INNER self that you must develop. It is your inner core that manifests outwardly through Masculine behaviors (or not).

What you need, rather than exhortations, is a **specific, objective framework you can use to guide the development of your Masculine core**. That is what I'll present to you now: the *Blueprint* for a new Masculine. One that is clear and replicable.

THE THREE ELEMENTS OF THE MASCULINE

Up until now, we've been speaking of masculinity in general terms. But you can't learn through generalities. So here I will lay out what I consider to be the **three primary elements of a Masculine core**:

1. Respond vs. React
2. Provide Structure
3. Create Safety

This framework distills out the essence of what's <u>underneath</u> the behaviors in the first list I shared. Rather than encouraging you to mimic them, I'm offering a specific framework for the inner work that will give rise to them organically. In any given moment, you can ask yourself, "*Am I being reactive, or choosing my response? Am I providing struc-*

ture? Am I making my woman feel physically, financially, or emotionally safe?" It becomes your checklist for instant self-diagnosis.

Let's now delve into each of the three elements of the *Masculin Blueprint*.

ELEMENT 1: RESPOND VS. REACT

This first one is the most important. Reactivity is at the root of so many non-Masculine behaviors, although not always in obvious ways. Consider for a moment the things you say, the ways you move or gesture, your facial expressions, the ways you react, the choices you make, the views you hold of yourself and others, all when you're in a stressful or triggering situation. Do these actions arise out of your conscious, considered choice? Or are they sometimes an unconscious reaction to external circumstances and your inner wounds?

Consider these questions in the context of your intimate relationship (for example, how you respond when your partner is angry and verbally attacking you), work situations (for example, how you operate in a contentious meeting), and even the most trivial interactions (such as how you walk through a crosswalk… I'll explain that one later). In the face of the stimuli in any of these situations, you either take in the information, make a choice, and consciously respond, or you react unconsciously based on habit or your fight or flight instincts.

There is a palpable difference between the two, and the people around you can feel it. The strong man considers and chooses. The weak man spends his life frantically reacting to the world and those around him.

To illustrate, let's look at a few of the situations from the list of non-Masculine behaviors that I shared earlier:

A REACTIVE MAN...	A MAN WHO RESPONDS...
...gets defensive when verbally attacked. He frantically tries to correct the "facts" in the other person's mind because he cannot tolerate being judged as "bad" or "wrong". He interrupts the other person and desperately tries to make his case so the other person won't be angry anymore.	...does not need to explain or defend. He holds space for the other's intense emotion and waits for them to finish before speaking. He acknowledges their feelings, may or may not choose to calmly correct a few facts, and apologizes if needed.
...withholds or changes his opinion in order to not conflict with others. He intensely or subtly fears angering others because he thinks it leads to rejection.	...speaks his truth. He respects others' viewpoints but feels comfortable with differences of opinion or method.
...withdraws when feeling hurt. He can't tolerate the hurt, nor use his curiosity to explore the other person's point of view. So he isolates himself in order to make the intense feelings stop.	...allows himself to feel the hurt, but instead of withdrawing he holds his ground and looks inward to examine what the hurt reveals about himself. He stays engaged and might even acknowledge that he feels hurt.
...gets unconsciously angry when being shamed. He hasn't come to grips with his own shame, so shaming by others touches a nerve. He unconsciously attacks back in order to make the pain stop and get the attention off of him.	...establishes a boundary with the other person that shaming is not acceptable, but otherwise stays open and in connection and invites the other person to share their needs or pain without shaming them.
...acts like a "nice guy". He smiles too much, tries to please everyone around him, defers to others. He calibrates his behavior to avoid upsetting anyone. And he hides the anger he feels as a result.	...does not orient himself around pleasing others. He lives his truth, knowing that others won't always like it. He is not narcissistic, but rather is at peace with who he is and what he does.

…**slouches while standing or sitting.** Poor posture is often rooted in fear. It is a self-protection mechanism against that fear. Subconsciously, it is a way to be more "invisible" in order to avoid trouble.

…has a natural upright posture. It is a reflection of his fearlessness and willingness to stand vulnerably in the world. He carries himself well because he is proud to be seen as who he is.

…**tries to initiate sex indirectly** by tentatively caressing his partner to assess if she is open to it. He is afraid to own his sexual desire out of fear of rejection.

…is in touch with his sexual desire and not afraid to openly express it to his partner. If she declines, he does not experience it as rejection.

…**gets nervous with a beautiful woman** or person of superior social status because he is unconsciously needing their approval or validation.

…does not need validation. He exists as who he is. There is no suspense or nervousness because his well-being is independent of the approval of others.

…**denies that he's feeling angry or scared**. He thinks these are signs of weakness, so he tries to hide them.

…owns his emotional state and doesn't shape his disclosures in reaction to outside approval.

…**moves and speaks rapidly**. These mannerisms are usually fueled by social anxiety, which comes from an intense need for others' approval.

…moves and speaks with ease and control at a measured pace. He's in touch with his physicality rather than lost in his head.

In every single case, the reactive man's behavior is an unconscious reaction to outside input. He's attempting to do one of several things:

- Bleed off the energy of anxiety
- Avoid being thought of as wrong or bad in some way
- Avoid rejection
- Avoid angering others
- Avoid his own feelings of fear or shame
- Avoid conflict

None of the reactive man's behaviors are actually chosen. None are rooted in his own desires and preferences. Rather, he orbits around everyone else's needs and opinions.

Viktor Frankl captured this poignantly when he wrote:

> *"Between stimulus and response there is a space. In that space is our power to choose our response. In our response lies our growth and our freedom."*

The reactive man does not allow himself this space to choose.

He doesn't *intend* to be this way. But a lifetime of unhealthy conditioning — trauma, poor family modeling, emotional neglect, etc. has put his nervous system on high alert.

In contrast, the Masculine man's nervous system is settled, even in the face of challenging stimuli. He consciously chooses his reactions, words, and movements. He takes outside input but is not thrown off course by it. He knows what he wants and pursues it, although hopefully without going to the extreme of excessive stubbornness, narcissism, or ego. He definitely does not go through life trying to please everyone else, though he may choose to serve others as he sees fit based upon his own values.

Intimate relationship is the most fertile ground for reactivity to be triggered. Work and unfamiliar social situations also rank high, but there's nothing quite like your woman being mad at you. And this is when the reactive man will find himself withdrawing (to get away from the pain of being with her anger), getting defensive (to try to correct facts so she will stop being mad), or contorting himself in sycophantic apology (thus giving up his own needs/views/motivations in order to avoid conflict). **He is reacting to her mood instead of operating out of choice**.

A man grounded in his Masculine core would not be doing this. Rather, he might hear her out and get curious about her angst. Or if she's being toxic, he may set a boundary. Or he might use humor to shake her out of an emotional tailspin. Whatever he does, he would be choosing it consciously.

Reactivity also shows up in many small ways that don't seem obvious at first. But other people can <u>feel</u> it. Without knowing exactly why, they may form an opinion that you are not a man in his power based on how you operate. I will give you an example. I recently watched a man walk through a crosswalk. When a car approached and slowed to a crawl about fifteen feet from that crosswalk, the man lifted his shoulders, hunched over a little, sped up his pace, and quickly shuffled across the street. Without words, his body language was saying *"Oh, sorry! I'll get out of your way. Sorry!"* Even though he was properly using the crosswalk and he had the right of way, he seemed to have an inner orientation that he shouldn't have been in the car's way, that the driver wanted him out of the way, and he was compulsively heeding that driver's unspoken need. There was no need for the pedestrian to act this way, but he did. He was operating purely out of a reaction to the input from the world. And he was silently screaming to the world *"I am not a man in my power!"*

A man grounded in his Masculine would have acted very differently. He would have kept going across the street, looked at the car, raised his hand with a polite gesture of thanks for slowing down, and proceeded on his way. His body language would have communicated that he had the right of way and knew it.

The reactive man in this example showed his true powerless nature without even realizing it. Without anyone having power over him in this situation, he put himself in the supplicant position. And he communicated it clearly through his actions.

This is just one example. But your inner state can show itself in any situation at any time. So you'll never be able to hide it or practice behaviors to cover all situations.

The only way to develop a solid Masculine core is inner work. Let the *Blueprint* be your guide in that work.

Now, what is it that causes you to be reactive? The external causes are too numerous to count, but I believe they can all be **distilled down into one <u>internal</u> common denominator: being in a state of threat**. Life circumstances arise which create a perception in you (whether conscious or subconscious) that something important is being threatened. It could be a physical threat. But, more likely these days, it is an emotional threat — being rejected, found unworthy or inadequate, ridiculed, shamed, slighted, forgotten, or abandoned. If these threats were to manifest, your subconscious believes you'd somehow lose love, connection, money, status, or safety.

As a result, your body-mind (which is a term I will use hereafter because your emotions manifest in both) will go into a threat state. The nervous system goes on overload and is flooded with the toxic energy of anxiety. You stop breathing. Your muscles clench. Your mind locks up. And you're no longer relaxed into the present moment.

It may sound ridiculous to your conscious mind, but that's the whole point — the subconscious works in some pretty illogical ways. These perceptions of threat are usually shaped and amplified by your childhood wounding.

This threat state can be intense, depending on the circumstances. But more likely it is mild and low-grade, almost hard to detect but still having a subtle impact on your behavior.

And your non-Masculine behaviors are the body-mind's way to cope with the anxiety you feel in this threat state. Go back to the earlier table of the "Reactive" vs. "Respond" behaviors. In each case, the reactive man is in some degree of a threat state and experiencing anxiety. His reactive behaviors are his subconscious ways to make it stop.

Sound complicated? Don't worry — we're going to dive deep on this in Chapter 8, as it is a major theme of the book.

In contrast to this, the man grounded in his Masculine core has a nervous system that is less susceptible. So the same stimuli don't affect him quite so intensely, and he is able to respond out of choice, rather than unconsciously reacting to the world around him.

Training your nervous system to handle intensity and anxiety is the path to becoming less reactive. I'll share various ways to do this later in Chapters 8–10.

ELEMENT 2: PROVIDE STRUCTURE

The second element of your Masculine core is the ability to provide structure for others. This means you do the work to reduce uncertainty, simplify and drive decisions, and create boundaries and processes for how things will get done.

When you do the research on possible vacation destinations, then propose three choices to your woman for discussion, you've reduced and simplified a decision for her. When you assertively guide the two of you to sit down and plan out the next few days so both of you know what's happening, that's providing structure. When you set a boundary during an argument that shaming won't be tolerated, that's providing structure. When you set a limit that your woman gets to bring only one suitcase on the trip because of the size of the rental car, and then help her make packing choices to fit, that's providing structure.

In each case, you're narrowing the wide-open scope of things, and then providing firm but fair pressure toward forward movement.

Your Masculine offering is to simplify the world's complexity for her. To reduce the confusion and stress that are inherent in life. To synthesize information and drive decisions. To orient everyone toward a goal and move things forward. It is the energy of the king or the good father — an organizing force that creates order from disorder. It sets direction and creates structure in which others can exercise their free will.

In contrast, the Feminine values connection over goal orientation. In those times when she chooses to be in her Feminine energy, she may be more open to following your lead rather than trying to navigate the world herself. Your ability to set direction and provide structure for her will help facilitate that.

In other words, when you're handling things, she can relax and blossom into her full openness and radiance, which is exactly the state in which you want her. This respite can be a deeply satisfying experience for a woman, particularly one who must exist in her own Masculine energy all day long at work. **Serving her in this way makes you uniquely attractive to her**.

If you want to embody this quality, you simply need to ask yourself in any given moment: "*How can I organize and clarify things for my woman?*" The order that you create becomes the fulcrum around which she can orient.

Let me give you an example of this dynamic. My woman and I were throwing a small party one night, but the truth was that I wasn't very excited about it. I had a lot of work to do and privately was wishing we hadn't planned it. So, I went a little passive on the morning of the party about what needed to get done that afternoon to prepare. I really just wanted to get on my computer and get to work, not talk about the party just yet. And, not surprisingly, my woman started to get a little agitated and unpleasant to be around, which of course just reinforced my impulse to lose myself in my computer. I took a shower, and during that break from working, I (thankfully) realized that my lack of commitment to the party was causing me to provide no direction to our effort. And this was having a significant impact on her. Knowing her well (and also confirming afterward), from her perspective it felt like she was being abandoned to think through all of the party prep on her own. With this insight, I emerged from the shower committed to the party. I went to the kitchen to find her and told her two things I would proactively get done that morning for the party, and I suggested a division of labor for the rest of the tasks. Her demeanor changed immediately. She softened, smiled, and said she felt closer to me. She said it wasn't just me "pitching in" that made her happier, but rather that I set some structure to our planning and started to lead us in the preparation.

It is true that she knew I was very busy, and she could have easily handled the prep on her own. But she would have been cranky the whole time. By simply adding a little structure to the whole process, I was able to "magically" turn a cranky girlfriend into a loving one.

Your clarity and decisiveness are the gift of the Masculine. Yes, this is a gift that you give her, not a burden that you must carry. Give it willingly.

And it is never about domineering or steamrolling others. As you'll see me write many times, this modern version of the Masculine is about clarity and leadership, not control. This includes becoming an organizing force for the world around you, a gravitational body around which others can orbit.

ELEMENT 3: CREATE SAFETY

This third element of the *Blueprint* involves doing what it takes to create a sense of safety in your woman. Most women will tell you that they must feel safe in order to settle and open to you. Creating safety for your woman frees her up to live as her best self. And it reinforces her trust in your leadership.

The three elements of safety that you will provide are financial, physical, and emotional.

In the financial domain is the archetype of the Provider. This doesn't mean you are the only one contributing (often both partners do), but she's not going to feel fully safe if you're not adequately contributing to your joint financial stability. She also won't feel safe if you overidentify with this Provider role by working too much at the exclusion of the family's or her needs.

Likewise, in the physical domain. Part of the Feminine psyche wants you to play the role of Protector against physical harm. This is more than just protecting her from a mugger. It could mean having fire extinguishers or an emergency kit in the event of a natural disaster. Or installing heavy deadbolts, cameras, and motion sensors to protect against home intrusion.

But in the rest of this chapter, we're going to focus on the Masculine role of creating emotional safety. Put simply, it means holding space for her to share her emotions without shame or fear, even if they are messy, unskillful, or aggressive. It is you standing strong and leading her back to her heart.

You know that a woman's emotions can be intense, particularly when they get directed at you. They can feel aggressive and confusing. But as illogical as they sometimes seem, they are absolutely 100 percent real to her. Yet, if she's being a mess, she usually knows it and **doesn't actually want to be in that state**. Take that in for a second. She doesn't actually want to be that way. It is not "just the way she is". It is not something you're "just supposed to stand there and take". She wishes she wasn't doing it, and she wishes you could lead her out of that state.

What she's craving from you is a safe space in which to let all of this messiness out. She wants permission to be illogical and convoluted. She wants to know that when she's like that, you won't turn and run, shut down, or shame her. That you will be her rock in the midst of her own emotional chaos, which is often even a mystery to her. That you will still love her and be there for her even after she shows you these messy parts. Even when it feels like she's blaming, shaming, and attacking you.

To do this, you must train your nervous system to handle the intensity so that you're responding and not reacting to her, which enables you to stay present and track her emotions. Rather than focusing on the aggression or drama, you're seeing deeper into the pain underneath. You know that she's at her worst when she feels the most scared, unsafe, or unloved.

Nearly every woman I know is craving this capacity in her man — to stand strong in the face of her chaos and lead her into a more loving and heartful state. We will discuss this in depth in Chapter 14.

Of course, this is far more easily said than done. When she's in that rageful/irrational/blaming/shaming place, it can blow your circuits out. If you're like most men, you'll go into a freeze state and not know what to do. Or take on a "hurt victim" mentality. Or want to run. It may feel like a burden to have to deal with it. You'll stay in your head and intellectualize. You might get defensive, or blaming, or angry. You might even question why you're in relationship with her.

And **the LAST thing you'll want to do, or feel capable of doing, is staying grounded and in connection with her.** But nonetheless that is what Masculine leadership requires.

I think it will help for me to share what this looks like with my woman. It starts with her upset with me for something I did or didn't do. She'll blast me with messy emotions, complete with plenty of blaming and shaming and showing disgust at my behavior. Instead of getting blown out, I try to settle my nervous system and stay present (Element 1 — being responsive rather than reactive), leaning on both my breath in the moment and my years of training my nervous system to handle intense Feminine energy. I also try to see her pain rather than the attack. I try to stay open to what she might be showing me rather than try to defend against something. Rather than freeze or withdraw (which are strong urges in the moment), I try to stay engaged.

From that grounded place, I may try to create a shift in the energy using one of the tools we'll discuss more in Chapter 14: holding space, humor, empathy, tickling, a hug, or even a boundary. I may simply ask her to share more of her pain. I might remind her of my love and commitment to her. I might offer empathy and reflect back what she's saying. I might even tease her to get her to see the ridiculousness of the intensity. Anything to get her out of her angry head and back into her heart and body. The Feminine is primarily a feeling creature, so she will be dysfunctional if she's trying to make sense of it all via her mind.

Of course, all of this is the exact OPPOSITE of what my body-mind screams at me to do. Let's face it — it is very challenging to have your partner angry and attacking you. Most men fail the test every time. Because it *is* a test, although she may not realize she's doing it: *"Can he handle my full emotional experience and still be there for me?"* She is seeing if you will step up, be her man, and contain her intense emotion. And when you fail that test, she stays in her mood, her angry attack mode, and her head.

There is a better way. You don't have to fail. Later you'll learn about the tools you can use to navigate these waters. You'll use them to break the tension, pull her out of her fury, and lead her back to her heart and body.

This is one of the MOST important things that a Masculine leader can do. After a few experiences of doing this, her trust in you will grow. The sense of emotional safety that she experiences with you will actually cause her to have fewer dysfunctional emotional outbursts going forward.

With you being the guardian of her financial, physical, and emotional safety, you'll find your woman's trust in you and devotion to you blossoming.

WHAT MASCULINITY IS NOT

Now that we've identified our *Blueprint* for a redefined Masculine, it will be illustrative to also look at some archetypes that are sometimes mistaken for masculinity.

One inaccurate belief is that masculinity is the sole domain of the tall, muscular guy who has the square jaw and confident smile. Because of his physicality, people will naturally assume this man has a well-developed Masculine core. But this is not always true. I've had plenty of experiences of meeting physically powerful men who turned out to have a weak energy. The contrast is striking.

A physically superior man isn't necessarily born with a settled nervous system, the capability and desire to provide structure, and the impulse to create safety for his woman. But his experience of the world has helped build his confidence. Over the course of his life, this man typically got whatever he wanted because of his looks and size. He intimidated the males and enticed the females. No one ever told the big guy "no" or ignored him. He doesn't even know what that would feel like, so his mind doesn't go to a place where he's fearful of these things happening. From this, his confidence and clarity were born. He rarely meets resistance, so he always assumes he'll get what he wants. So, while his looks and size are a huge boost for him, it is the resultant mindset that developed within him over time that is the core of his Masculine energy. But it is also true that ANY man can develop this mindset, even if he doesn't possess exceptional size and looks. I know this to be true. A professor of mine back in graduate school was five foot six, yet I have a distinct memory of him withstanding the verbal attack of an angry and aggressive graduate student while giving a public talk, then verbally neutralizing her aggression by staying settled and setting a boundary.

I remember meeting another man at a workshop who was five foot four and balding, yet because of the force of his personal energy, he occurred to me as much larger. I asked him point-blank if he knew why that was, and he told me it was because he'd practiced Krav Maga, an intense and violent Israeli martial art, for about ten years and it had changed him profoundly. Neither of these men was physically impressive in any way, yet simply because of their energy I was drawn to them — and sure that I'd rather be their friend than their rival.

The reality is that, short of jaw implants, elevator shoes, and steroids, you aren't going to transform yourself into being a hunk. So your path to a strong Masculine core is going to have to start from the inside. My guidance to you is to stop worrying about what you don't have and focus on the teachings I will share with you in this book.

And while you're at it, stop assuming that physically imposing men with whom you come into contact are Masculine. These projections only give them undeserved power over you.

• • •

Another false version of masculinity is the man who lives life emotionally and physically tightened up. You know the type. It shows in the way he walks. Usually, the upper body is held very tightly. The arms don't swing naturally, the torso doesn't rotate. The head doesn't move and the jaw is clenched. It's as if he is doing a military march.

Emotionally, he is reserved to the point of being shut down. He's always "fine", even in situations that would naturally elicit emotion from any normal human. He dismisses emotion as something for weak men and women. Others may respect him or even be a little afraid of him. But they won't feel connected to him.

He is not grounded in real personal power, but rather just contracted in self-protection. He is really just bracing against a fear which he doesn't even acknowledge to himself.

I have compassion for this man. He's condemned himself to a life of clenching. To maintaining a false front of untouchability. And this type of tightness will prevent any real sort of emotional connection with others. This is going to be a real problem in intimate relationship. Even if the man is handsome, smart, and successful, women will eventually tire of his lack of emotional vulnerability (a topic we will discuss further in Chapter 9).

• • •

Another prominent archetype is that of the "Alpha Dog". This is not the same as our definition of a Masculine leader. An Alpha Dog is unquestionably in charge. He dominates others with little regard for their feelings. Everyone else is expected to fall in line. The Alpha often gains his position through superior physicality, intellect, or aggression.

Yet masculinity as I present it is not predicated on being superior or more aggressive. It is about purging your own anxiety and fear, making choices instead of reacting, setting direction, and taking care of others. The degree to which you are "in charge" is based on how grounded you are and how well you inspire trust from those around you, particularly your woman. The Alpha Dog fights his way to the top. But the truly

Masculine man naturally rises to the top as others see him living the qualities outlined in the *Blueprint*.

• • •

Similar to the Alpha Dog is the archetype of the Asshole. He does what he wants and doesn't seem to care what others think. Like it or not, women seem to be attracted to the Asshole-type, which is, of course, so confusing to men. They ask themselves, *"Do I need to act like a jerk to date beautiful women?"* Thankfully for everyone, the answer is no. You see, the Asshole archetype doesn't last very long in relationship because his act gets old fast. He typically lacks care and respect for others, and doesn't have the relating skills necessary for long-term relationship.

But he does have one special quality that women crave in a man: he lives fearlessly by his own rules. As a result, he's not needy. He is not tentative because he knows what he wants. Through their way of being, both the Alpha Dog and the Asshole communicate that they strongly believe in themselves. **They attract others to them because they believe themselves to be powerful, and therefore others believe they are powerful**.

Of course, the Alpha Dog and Asshole usually are this way because they are narcissists who are not capable of considering the needs of others. That's not masculinity. It's just a serious character flaw that wears thin quickly. But power and narcissism often manifest together, and are frequently confused for one another. Women often get fooled by these archetypes, only to later suffer from the self-focus and callousness that they mistook for powerful, Masculine energy. But women will tolerate a lot just to get an experience of a man who lives by his own code.

• • •

The final archetype I will share is something I call the Righteous Supplicant. His version of masculinity is apologizing profusely for the sins of all males. A proud nice guy. He wants to be a "good man" and fully honor women, and wears it like his own badge of honor. Each Righteous Supplicant tries to one-up the others in his repudiation of "bad Masculine behavior".

Of course I support the goal of honoring women — it is woven throughout this work. But it is the Righteous Supplicant's intention behind his behavior which I dislike because it doesn't feel like a position taken by choice, but rather a reaction out of guilt, shame, or a desire to be a "good boy for mommy". A Masculine man does not honor women in order to gain their approval. He does it because that is who he is and how he chooses to live.

I recently saw a video by a clothing company on the topic of masculinity. The title of the video referred to the need to evolve the definition of what "Masculine" means, which is a notion I fully support — this whole book is about redefining what it means to be in your Masculine. But when the commercial proceeded to show various men repudiating Masculine qualities such as "powerful", and then try to redefine the Masculine as "whatever I decide to be", "being honest", or "just being human", that is where they lost me. The Masculine IS powerful. And I don't believe it's just about "being honest" or any other generic phrase. Nor is it about "just being human", because that suggests we're all exactly the same. The Masculine that I believe in is about exhibiting the core qualities I've described in the *Blueprint*, no matter how exactly they manifest or in which gender.

I deeply believe that the Masculine CAN be a force for good in the world, one that I will not repudiate. And I hope you won't either.

• • •

Each of these archetypes tends to focus on one of the elements of masculinity at the expense of the other two. The man who lives tightly over-focuses on "Respond vs. React". He's so clenched and shut down that he reacts to nothing, including others' emotional needs. The Alpha/Asshole over-focuses on "Provide Structure" because he wants to dominate everyone. This is toxic masculinity. And the Righteous Supplicant over-focuses on "Create Safety" — he tries so hard to be completely non-threatening (the classic "nice guy") but forgets to provide the leadership that many women are craving.

The true Masculine man lives all three of these elements. In doing that, he models a life of being both in his power and in his heart.

• • •

I have one final thought on this topic to share. If you talk too much about your intention to "lead" more, you may experience a lot of resistance from the world because of implied connotations and projections of misogyny. It may also create resistance in your strong woman. So, let me simplify this for you: never TALK about leading or Masculine leadership. Just LIVE the *Blueprint*. That's all you have to do. Put all three elements into daily practice and you'll find yourself organically bringing more leadership to your relationship.

CONCLUSION

The three elements presented form the foundation of your Masculine core. My goal is that the *Blueprint* makes this process more tangible and actionable for you. If you want to know how your own Masculine energy stacks up, ask yourself: "*Do I respond or do I react when in stressful interpersonal situations? Do I provide structure for those around me? And, do I create safety for those who are important to me?*" I encourage you to scrutinize your daily way of being through this lens. The Feminine, which we will explore in the next chapter, tends to open when you manifest these elements in your life and close when you don't.

CHAPTER 6

THE FEMININE

Let's now turn our attention to the Feminine state. A full exploration is out of the scope of this work. Nonetheless, I will share my experience of the Feminine as a way to contrast it with the Masculine.

And, as a reiteration of what I've said before, the "Feminine" does not equate to "female". It describes an energy and set of qualities. Yes, in the chosen scope of this particular book, we are associating it with your female partner. But that is not a universal characterization.

TRAITS OF THE FEMININE

I will start with some experiential impressions of the woman in my life, who happens to have a very Feminine essence. The Feminine is light; I picture my woman's radiant smile and laugh and the way they lift my spirits. It is beauty (which is in the eye of the beholder, and can be inner or outer), and I envision her slender form, which both entrances and arouses me. The Feminine can surrender to the Masculine lead; I imagine how she allows me to guide her body in the bedroom. It is change, and I'm reminded of her many moods that shift so quickly and seamlessly. The Feminine is movement; I envision the intoxicating way her body moves on the dance floor. It is heart-based; I'm grateful for all of the ways she shows me hers and reminds me to find mine. The Feminine is a fierce defender of our connection; she shows me the raw pain she feels when my avoidance, fear, or lack of presence interferes with it. The Feminine is nurturing; I remember all the ways she skillfully heals and replenishes me. And the Feminine is expressive; I recall the way her face comes alive and voice gets animated when she tells a story or shares her feelings.

These energies of hers feed and uplift me in so many ways. David Deida often says that the Masculine is all about work, struggle, and achievement. The Feminine gives it something to live for, puts the color in what would otherwise be a gray life of striving. I agree with that.

Admittedly, I have shared a more poetic description of the Feminine. So here are some of the more practical attributes I've observed with women in their Feminine energy. A woman in this state might:

- Care about beauty over utility, and thus might opt to wear a pretty dress rather than pants or sweats
- Exhibit a softness and ease, in contrast to the get-it-done furrowed brow look that she might carry around at work
- Be able to provide a nurturing energy by knowing ways to ease my stress, worry, or fatigue from my worldly pursuits
- Have an inner glow that radiates out through her smile and laugh
- Be in touch with her body, and capable of moving it in seductive ways
- Be open to following your lead rather than endlessly challenging you
- Trust you (assuming you've earned it) rather than criticize you'

- Deeply desire a heart connection with you that goes beyond physical attraction, pragmatic partnering, and having fun together
- Fiercely tend to the flow of love between you two, including calling you out to be your best self when your behavior interferes

None of these are ways that a woman SHOULD be. Rather, they are simply my own observations of what Feminine energy can look like. To a man who chooses to identify as Masculine, a woman in her Feminine is a LOT more enjoyable. She piques your interest and inspires you to take care of her and be a better man in general. The interesting part is that YOU have the power to put her into this state. You being grounded in your Masculine core will enable her to relax and open. The Feminine comes out when she feels loved and led by you.

In the domain of intimacy (this does not apply in professional environments) I'm far more attracted to a woman who has a Feminine side. I don't want her in that state all of the time. But I'd like it to be a core part of her. And, speaking bluntly, I'm not as attracted to a woman who's always in her Masculine energy. I can respect and like her. I can enjoy her physical beauty. I can appreciate her intelligence and capability. But sustained attraction probably won't be there.

Not all women have access to their Feminine side. Some are wholly committed to providing their own lead for themselves, all of the time. Some are too wounded or shut down to relax and open. Some simply have no idea what being Feminine means. And some are indignant about it, believing that being "Feminine" as I describe it means being weak and archaic. These are all choices that she can make. You can't demand that it be different. But you can invite her into her Feminine through your way of being.

AREN'T WE EQUAL PARTNERS?

Now, some of you may be wondering why you want her to follow your lead. You may tell yourself that you like a capable woman and that you are OK with the two of you always being "equal partners". Again, this is a choice you can make. But be aware of where that road leads: both of you waiting for the other to lead. Rather than ever being bold, you simply wait for her to express her preferences and then adopt that as the direction. Meanwhile, down at the biological level she's wanting you to show some leadership once in a while. And thus you deny her the gift of your Masculine direction by never providing structure, leaving her to make all her own decisions, and leaving her to solve all of her emotional problems.

And you wonder why she's a bit edgy rather than soft with you. It's because she's continually stuck in her Masculine energy.

Sure, when times are good, it's fine and you have a partner in life. **But when things get tough, you have a RIVAL.** With both of you in your Masculine, you'll start butting heads. She may start questioning your decisions. Not just once, but consistently, relentlessly. Unless you are absolutely more competent than her in every way, always one step ahead, she'll find something to resist when she's in her Masculine.

Does this sound too pessimistic? Don't count on it. When you add the stresses of two jobs, the familiarity challenge of long-term relationship, or the addition of kids, this is quite common.

And if your woman is second-guessing you and constantly telling you what to do, it is not going to feel good to you as a man. It can be tiring. At that point, you have three choices. One is to surrender to her lead and become emasculated. The second is to fight back, and that generally leads to a horrible relationship or a parting of ways. And, your third option is to become the Masculine leader she craves. No, that doesn't mean "just being in charge". It means offering your lead while incorporating all of her own input, capability, and wisdom. All in service of inviting her back into her Feminine energy and those delectable Feminine behaviors that you love.

Remember, it is not your divine right to be the leader — you need to earn it. And, of course, it is a woman's sole choice on how much she wants to be in her Feminine. All you can do is step into your power, offer your lead, and earn her trust. The rest will happen organically.

A woman's power and her Feminine are not mutually exclusive. She need not give up the former to exude the latter. As a man, I can tell you it is an absolute treat to be with a woman who chooses to be both fully in her power *and* her Feminine. Unfortunately, it is a rarity (just as it is rare for a woman to meet a good man who is also grounded in his Masculine).

Surprisingly, in my own life, I've found it is often the older women who are beginning to hunger for a strong male presence in their lives so they can relax into their Feminine. They spent their twenties and thirties pursuing career and empowerment, only to find in their forties and beyond a craving for the occasional experience of Polarity as well. That is not intended to be an accurate representation of women as a whole — it's just a reflection of what I've observed in women I know.

Do you want her in her Feminine 100 percent of the time? No, that is not the goal here. The energy is delightful in doses, but real life intrudes and she'll need to be capable of taking care of her worldly responsibilities. But in those times that the two of you choose to create Polarity, you will find the full Feminine to be very intoxicating.

POWERFUL + FEMININE = INTIMIDATING

But beware: radiant, Feminine energy in a woman can sometimes be intimidating. Like moths to light, men are irresistibly drawn to her, but frightened of her at the same time. The more in her Feminine she is, the more she'll show you her wild, raw heart. The more she'll express her deepest pain and expect you to hold space for it.

Frankly, in the domain of intimacy, **you rarely get the radiance without the "crazy".** Yes — the irrational, illogical, unpredictable, angry, unstoppable side of women that absolutely confounds you is all part of the Feminine. Frankly, **you don't get the radiance without the crazy.**

In that state, she'll verbally attack you and push all the right buttons to upset you. She can be irrational, so you struggle to find a way to even respond. She twists the truth just enough to make you seem like the bad guy, and makes conclusions about your behavior that may almost fit the facts but don't match your intentions at all. She brings up things from years ago. And she jumps around between multiple issues and intertwines them, so you don't even know where to begin in responding. Her anger brings up your fears of rejection. Your sweet little kitten turns into a raging monster in a nanosecond. Sound familiar? We've all been there. It's painful, but par for the course with any woman who has even a little bit of spirit to her.

So, in your pursuit of a relationship with a truly Feminine woman, I say be careful what you wish for. You'd better bring your A-game.

CONCLUSION

The core Feminine is nurturing care and wild radiance, in contrast to your Masculine stillness. At times she'll feel alien to you. Loving one minute, attacking the next. Change is constant in the Feminine, balanced exquisitely by your groundedness.

With this understanding of both Masculine and Feminine, let's now look at the dance between the two. This is Polarity, and is what we'll discuss in the next chapter.

CHAPTER 7

POLARITY

Polarity is the dance between the Masculine and the Feminine. It is the magic that happens when the two poles meet. In this chapter, we will look more closely at this dynamic and how it explains why your Masculine leadership is so critical to a successful relationship.

ANCIENT BEGINNINGS

The concept of Polarity has existed for thousands of years. Ancient Hindu tradition speaks of Shiva and Shakti, symbols of two very different energies. Shakti is the Feminine embodiment of energy, while Shiva represents the Masculine and is said to symbolize pure Consciousness. In this Hindu tradition, "Consciousness" refers to the unchanging and unswayable Masculine observer. This is exactly what we've been talking about — the Masculine being unmoved by the challenges of life, whether they be his woman's anger, business competition, or a challenge from another man.

This is not to say that he's not affected, nor that he's indifferent. Rather, he maintains that gap between stimulus and response. He observes without being scared off, getting lost in anxiety, or becoming reactive. He then consciously chooses how he will respond. That is what is meant by the "unchanging and unswayable observer". He is a rock in the midst of his woman's and the world's chaos.

Tradition tells us that Shiva and Shakti originated in the splitting of the One Consciousness at the beginning of Creation. Since then each has been constantly striving to reunite with the other. They need each other. Energy on its own can produce nothing; Consciousness gives it form and direction. Likewise, Consciousness without energy is dormant power, and on its own is unable to create anything. It is only when Shiva and Shakti are united that action and creation arise. This very much describes the Masculine and Feminine, in whichever gender they manifest.

Many spiritual traditions talk about Consciousness, and a common element between all of them is the notion of having "two selves". One is the "self" that lives in and deals with daily life. The other "self" lies deeper, aware of everything but not caught up in the drama. It is an impassive observer. Many well known spiritual masters describe this concept:

- Ramana Maharshi talks about the "real Self", which is an unchanging state of awareness rather than an individual "I". It is not caught in the drama of life.
- Eckhart Tolle talks about the part of you that is the "Watcher" of your own thoughts and feelings but does not get lost in their chaos.
- Gary Zukov talks of the Soul, which is the unchanging part of you that is separate from your personality through which you interface with daily life.

- Leonard Jacobson talks about the "awakened Presence" inside of you, which is different than the "person you have become".

These teachers inspire us to find that place within ourselves which transcends the moment by moment chaos of the world and our minds. From that place, we can become the unchanging and unswayable observer. We can become Shiva. From this place of calm observation, we can <u>choose</u> how to act. This is a powerful place from which to live one's life. **It is not passivity — it is living from intention and choice.**

The Feminine, as embodied in the concept of Shakti, is very different. She symbolizes energy — manifesting as connection, change, rawness, abundance, and nurturing. How might this look in the real world? On the positive side, it manifests as a radiant woman — full of life, prone to smile and laugh, very animated. But it also shows itself in darker ways, some of which you might experience as "crazy". In the mythology of Polarity, this is embodied by Kali — the goddess waiting to chop off the head of any man who is less than fully conscious.

Take heart. You can weather these storms, and learn to completely diffuse them in a way that has her actually trusting you <u>more</u> afterward. It is your Masculine leadership which will ground and settle her. And when you do this, the nagging abates. The attacking abates. The crazy abates.

This is Polarity. This is where Masculine and Feminine complement and fulfill each other. And this is when things get a whole lot more fun.

NATURAL BUT SCARY

Part of Polarity's magic is the simplicity of resting in one's natural energy state. In daily life, both men and women exhibit a mix of both Masculine and Feminine energies. But when you are cultivating Polarity, a couple (with a Masculine-identified man and a Feminine-identified woman) can each relax into their ONE primary energy. A man in his Masculine is freed to manifest his primal, proactive nature. A woman in her Feminine can surrender and not have to make choices. Resting in your ONE primary energy, without having to balance a mix of the two within you, can be deeply nourishing.

But Polarity can scare some people. Let's be clear — it has an implied power differential at its core. In the domain of gender relations, we have a dark history here. In her book *Mating In Captivity*, author Esther Perel says:

> *"The poetics of sex, however, are often politically incorrect, thriving on power plays, role reversals, unfair advantages, imperious demands, seductive manipulations, and subtle cruelties. American men and women, shaped by the feminist movement and its egalitarian ideals, often find themselves challenged by these contradictions. We fear that playing with power imbalances in the sexual arena, even in a consensual relationship between mature adults, risks overthrowing the respect that is essential to human relationships."*

Much of Perel's book is about this primary contradiction in our intimacy — that love seeks safety, closeness, and security, while erotic desire seeks mystery, edginess, and unpredictability. We strive for the former and then years later wonder why we bore each other. In cultivating our Polarity, we feed our erotic desire. The Masculine gets to revel in his power a little more, the Feminine rides the unpredictable currents of surrender. **In playing with Polarity, we're choosing to give up the belief that we're all the same all the time.**

Certainly, American culture may be more resistant to this than other cultures. Perel goes on to say:

> " … egalitarianism, directness, and pragmatism are en-
> trenched in the American culture and inevitably influence
> the way we think about and experience love, and sex. Lat-
> in Americans' and Europeans' attitude towards love, on the
> other hand, tend to reflect other cultural values, and are
> more likely to embody the dynamic of seduction, the focus
> on sensuality, and the idea of complementarity (i.e. being
> different but equal) rather than absolute sameness."

Other cultures have managed to keep Polarity the norm in their intimacy. This is not to say this is a better way, because those same coun-
tries also tend to lag behind America in women's rights. If only we
could evolve into the best of both worlds.

That is what the *Blueprint* hopes to foster. A way of being with your
woman that respects her while incorporating seduction and Polarity.

Despite many women expressing this desire to surrender into their
Feminine more, it is still tricky territory. The risk is that admitting to
this desire would somehow give tacit approval for male dominance in
all the other arenas of life. But Perel offers hope as she writes:

> "…prisoners rarely have the desire to pretend they are pris-
> oners. Only the free can choose to make believe. To my
> thinking, being able to play with roles goes some way to-
> ward indicating that you're no longer controlled by them."

It is the increasing levels of equality we have achieved that makes it
safer for Polarity to re-emerge. Unlike the compulsory nature of things
throughout history, this will be a very different arrangement: it will be

by *choice*. The Masculine-identified person offers their lead. The Feminine-identified person chooses whether to accept it.

So, if you find your woman irritable, nagging you, criticizing you, or not open to sex, don't blame her or run away. Create Polarity. Ground yourself in your Masculine and induce her into her Feminine. Stop waiting for her to change. The key to things being different starts with you alone. This is Masculine leadership.

And what does this look like in real life? It is simply the manifestation of the three elements of the *Blueprint*. You're grounded in the face of her intense emotion (Chapters 8–10). You're providing direction and structure for her in life and in the bedroom (Chapters 11–13). And you're helping her feel safe (Chapter 14–15). When you do these things, she relaxes.

No longer do you need to be confounded by your woman's occasional irritable, nagging, cold, or irrational behavior. No longer should you blame HER, thinking that it is HER behavior that SHE needs to fix. You now know that you can LEAD her out of that behavior via your Masculine leadership.

She will be drawn to the man that can do that for her.

THE FEMININE'S ROLE

Now, one final thought about the Feminine's role in this dance. Men often ask me, "*You're coaching ME to be the solution, but what about her? What does SHE need to be doing?*" This is a legitimate question. Should the Masculine partner be expected to do all of the work here?

Here is what I tell my clients: **you may or may not be the problem, but you ARE the solution**. Keep your focus on what YOU can do to induce your woman into her Feminine. Blaming her and waiting for her to change or fix something are all simply distractions from what you need to do.

David Deida and others in his lineage taught me something that helped me make sense of this dynamic. He helped me see that the Feminine's role is not to figure out how to be less emotional and more rational. It is not to do her own deep inner work to fix her issues (although you hope she is self-motivated to do this). It is not to think the way that we think. It is not to keep her word. That's just you projecting your Masculine way of seeing the world onto her. Rather, **the primary Feminine responsibility is to reflect back to you where you are not caring for her, where you are not in your heart, where you are out of integrity, and where you are not conscious or present**. David's phrase for this role is that of "Oracle". She is your Oracle who shows you these blind spots.

But, unfortunately, her expression can be messy. She is a feeling creature, so these things that she experiences with you can occur as pain in her heart and body. And, her expression of this pain through her cognitive mind often comes in the form of complaint, bitchiness, insults, shaming, withdrawal, and sexual shutdown. They are all simply dysfunctional expressions of her heart.

That is where you can help. By handling the feelings of threat and anxiety within you that inevitably occur when her expression is toxic, you'll stay grounded. From this place, you can hold space and create some emotional safety for her. Then you can lead her back to her heart, which longs to feel closer to you, feel loved by you, and feel led and protected by you. Again, we'll talk more about all of this in Chapter 14.

This is a powerful reframe that has made a big difference in my own life. Where I used to get defensive or dismissive when my woman would complain, I now give her the benefit of the doubt (initially) and try to see it as her being my Oracle, reflecting back to me some way I'm not being present, heartful, or a leader. I pause and ask myself "*What could be true here?*" rather than immediately resist or defend. This does NOT mean that she gets a free pass on bad behavior, or that I agree with whatever she says. But I do open to her Feminine gift of intuitive insight. More times than not, there is something there that I need to see about myself. And for the times that she's truly off, I can then consciously (not reactively) choose to clarify, set a boundary, or engage in an examination of the issue with her.

With this simple change in mindset, I'm far less defensive. By simply accepting that **there is wisdom in the Feminine, beyond what my Masculine nature can sense**, I'm much more relaxed when my woman complains.

Ironically, she also changed as a result of this realization I had. She sees greater space for her emotional expression, for her Feminine input. She knows that it is sometimes clumsy and messy, and feels safer now that she sees me making space for it. Knowing this, she organically "acts up" less. It is not a conscious choice on her part — it just seems to happen.

So to my clients, I say let her be your Oracle and show you where you're off. Stop waiting for her to fix herself. Stop waiting for her to change. Stop waiting for her to always be rational. Learn to be grateful for her clumsy expression. Learn to see it as a gift rather than an attack or burden. Respond with Masculine leadership and create Polarity. You will see your relationship radically change for the better.

CONCLUSION

Polarity is a dance that is essential to keeping the juice alive in your relationship. It is the key to escaping the Gordian knot of a relationship that has gone flat, combative, or contemptuous. Your key takeaway here is that you CAN affect the situation. Polarity is a powerful force that you can harness and guide toward opening your woman up when she's at her worst. Any man that wishes to be in relationship with a juicy woman will need to master this skill.

ELEMENT 1

RESPOND VS. REACT

In this section, we will dive into the first element of the Blueprint. "Respond vs. React" refers simply to that quality of interacting with the world from a place of choice rather than from unconscious reaction.

At the root of all reactivity lies a feeling of threat which creates anxiety that can significantly affect your behavior. We do a deep dive on this in Chapter 8.

Then both of the subsequent chapters explore how to train yourself to handle intensity. Chapter 9 seeks to help you establish a better relationship to your emotions in order to reduce reactivity. And in Chapter 10, I'll share embodiment exercises that you can use to train your nervous system over time to handle more intensity.

CHAPTER 8

THREAT

A sense of threat is at the root of all of your non-Masculine behaviors. These behaviors are just your body-mind's way of bleeding off or avoiding the unpleasant energy of anxiety that arises in this state.

Without a doubt, understanding and taming your anxiety should be the highest priority in your quest to restore your Masculine core. It will yield profound organic change in your way of being.

I can't emphasize this topic enough — threat is THE central issue with which you need to deal relative to developing your Masculine core. In the worldview I am sharing with you, everything boils down to this.

ANXIETY IS YOUR ENEMY

No one consciously chooses to manifest the reactive behaviors I listed in Chapter 5. They just happen unconsciously. You may or may not even be aware that you're exhibiting them.

You would, of course, prefer to suppress these behaviors. But no matter how much willpower you apply, it's impossible to do so in any sustainable way by focusing on the behavior itself. You just can't predict or prepare for the infinite combinatorials of circumstances and stimuli which will trigger you. You would just be chasing symptoms rather than addressing the underlying problem.

The good news is that you don't have to. That is because of one simple maxim which is a core principle of this book: **nearly all non-Masculine behaviors are rooted in one thing — threat.**

The chain of logic is simple: in life, you inevitably encounter challenging circumstances. Sometimes those circumstances can feel like they threaten something important to you: physical safety, resources, reputation, connection, love, respect, career status or trajectory, or self-image. More often than not, old wounding, shame, fear, or any form of underdevelopment in you will amplify this feeling into a genuine sense of threat, even if it is subtle and still at the level of your subconscious. Anxiety is the body-mind's response to this sense of threat. It occurs as an unpleasant energy in the body. Your non-Masculine behaviors are your body-mind's way of coping with the intensity of this anxiety.

Some examples could include:

- Your woman is mad at you, and her displeasure triggers your fear that she will think less of you or even leave you. It feels like a threat to the relationship. This creates anxiety, so you meekly cave into her demands so that her displeasure, and therefore the anxiety, stop.
- You subconsciously covet the approval of your CEO, or possibly a beautiful woman. Their validation subconsciously matters a lot to you, and the prospect of not achieving it threatens your sense of self-worth. So you end up talking too much in conversation

with them because you're trying too hard to win that validation/approval.

- Someone is criticizing something you've done. Your subconscious mind fears being thought poorly of because it believes this leads to being rejected, which threatens your sense of belonging and of being respected. So you end up getting defensive in order to avoid the criticism and thus retain your sense of self-worth.

In each case above, your subconscious fears some form of rejection. Your wounds amplify the sense of threat and make the stakes seem far higher than reality would dictate, and so anxiety kicks in. Then your subconscious creates behaviors to make the anxiety go away or help you numb it out. Sadly, this rarely ever works.

Admittedly, this is an oversimplification of a complex issue. But in my worldview, it covers <u>most</u> of the reasons a man is not in his power, and thus provides a useful framework for you to develop yourself. Instead of chasing your tail trying to eliminate or mimic behaviors, you'll instead train your nervous system to cope with threat and anxiety.

I feel clear about this theme because I experienced it firsthand. I still face Feminine intensity and worldly challenges in my life. But I did the work to train and settle my nervous system over that time, and somehow those same stressors seem so much more manageable now. The world didn't change. I just became more grounded, and the world organically became easier. I operate more out of choice and less out of a compulsion to end the intensity. It means **I'm able to live more from intention than reaction**.

But it is not an easy journey for anyone because the roots of this vexing dynamic are buried very deeply in your psyche, and are usually based on early childhood wounding.

EARLY WOUNDING

This wounding starts early in life. Children are very emotionally vulnerable in their first twelve years of life. Many will encounter certain events which may seem normal but can actually be rather traumatic: being hungry for an extended period, crying too long in a crib, a parent not keeping commitments, an angry/disinterested/disappointed parent, etc. Some will experience overtly traumatic emotional or physical abuse. I think of all of these types of experiences as "Disconnection Events", and they imprint fear onto children's susceptible nervous systems. They end up feeling hyper-vulnerable, abandoned, alone, invalidated, not protected, not taken care of, or disconnected from the parent. These are not cognitive thoughts, but rather just primal feelings.

This was effectively illustrated in something called the "Still-Face Experiment". Dr. Edward Tronick filmed a mother playing with her baby, with liberal cooing and smiling. Then, as scripted by the experiment, the mother stops responding to the baby and just stares at her for two minutes, stony-faced. The baby unsuccessfully tries to get the mother to engage. As this continues, the baby grows more and more distraught, eventually beginning to scream and cry. Clearly, babies viscerally and acutely respond to disconnection.

Going further, because children are naturally so egocentric, they come to irrationally see these Disconnection Events as their fault. When these bad things happen, it must be a result of the child doing something wrong and displeasing the parent.

Putting the two together, many children develop two beliefs. The first is that others' displeasure with or lack of attention on them is *their* fault. The second is that others' displeasure with or disinterest in them will inevitably lead to feeling rejected, lonely, or abandoned, states in which they experienced an intolerable fear. Tragically, **this mindset predisposes the child to readily believe it is he who must change in order to avoid others' displeasure and its consequences.**

For many people, this **fear irrationally persists into adulthood, often in the form of a strong reluctance to disappoint others**. As ridiculous as it may sound, your nervous system sometimes responds to adult-era stimuli (such as someone being displeased with you) as if you were still a vulnerable infant or child experiencing Disconnection Events. It amplifies your sense of threat, thus increasing your defensiveness, feelings of hurt, impulse to withdraw, or impulse to smooth everything over. Despite your best intentions, you respond from a wounded place rather than from a grounded place.

Apply this lens to the examples I gave earlier in this chapter. In each case, there is a strong reticence to disappoint or displease others.

MEN RESIST

Men typically resist this notion. The "*Oh, don't start talking to me about my childhood!*" skepticism is pretty common. Men want to be pragmatic and assume everything happens because of here-and-now circumstances.

I used to be that way as well. It took me about a year of post-divorce therapy for my therapist to finally discover my own childhood trauma. When she did, it was an "*Aha!*" moment because it explained so much about some of my dysfunctional adult behaviors. Three days after I was born, my mother was diagnosed with serious melanoma. She had major surgery days later, and her doctor gave her a 15 percent chance to live. She was bedridden in recovery, unable to even lift her arms for six weeks. As heroic as my father was to care for her and my brother and me, it would have been impossible for Baby Me to get the level of care and attention I needed. I spent many hours in a crib or bouncy seat, demanding but not receiving enough attention. Baby Me reached out for others and they were not always there. My parents were dealing both with my mother's acute physical limitations as well as the strong potential that she would not survive. It was not their fault, nor a result of neglect. It was simply the cards we were dealt at the time.

My therapist helped me see the effect on my own psyche. How Baby Me subconsciously felt abandoned and therefore experienced panic at times. And how Adult Me has felt panic at breaks in connection within important relationships. It was my infantile fear of being "abandoned" arising in my adult life. I came to see how this explained some of my more vexing behaviors that played a role in the breakdown of my marriage.

I now understand that those behaviors had their origins in the first few months of my life. And I now see the negative impact on my own Masculine power: I would relinquish my needs, my truth, and my voice in order to avoid breaks in connection with others. The stakes were just too high because they were amplified by my childhood wounds.

This childhood experience was not the only factor shaping these behaviors of mine. But it was a contributor.

I've put in the time to explore and deeply heal these wounds, and I've experienced profound personal changes as a result. I believe all of this is possible for *you*, which is why we are exploring this topic. This is critically important for you to explore because, in my worldview, our childhood wounding is the most plausible explanation for our irrational, non-Masculine behaviors.

It starts by acknowledging that EVERY child has experienced Disconnection Events to varying degrees. It need not have a dramatic storyline like physical abuse or a parent walking out on the family. It happens even with the most well-meaning and dedicated parents. Raising children is hard and exhausting. Parents lose patience no matter how much they love their kids. The calm late-middle-aged parents you see today were more than likely occasional raving lunatics back when they were struggling to raise you. Every parent of young children is exhausted and stretched too thin at times. And in that state, they don't always treat their kids the way they intend to treat them. You might feel some resistance to this notion because it feels like an implicit indictment of your parents. It's not. More than likely they did their best. But it does support the notion that even YOU have some degree of an abandonment and disconnection dynamic in you.

INTO ADULTHOOD

Unfortunately, this compulsion to avoid others' displeasure gets burned into the nervous system, surviving intact into adulthood. When your adult self feels threat, your nervous system can still unconsciously behave as if you're a child, mortally dependent on keeping others happy so they don't "abandon" or "disconnect" from you and precipitate the panic that your subconscious remembers all too well. **This fear dynamic usually has little to do with the present**. It is simply the nervous system reacting to current events as if you were still as helpless as you were in childhood.

I see examples all around me. I have a close friend who had a childhood history of stuttering, and his parents did not give him the emotional support he needed throughout the vulnerable years of his childhood. He cites this as one major factor contributing to the powerful social anxiety he feels as an adult.

Sometimes, the specific connection between childhood wounds and today's behaviors are not obvious. This is the case with another close friend of mine who is a major "pleaser" in relationship. When I showed him a draft of the first few chapters of this book, he said: "*I feel like it was written specifically about me.*" Yet he consistently rejects any connection to his childhood, which he described as "normal" and "fine". Now, it is not for me to second guess him, but what I do know is that some of his behaviors are VERY hard to explain. The way he has a twenty-year pattern of tolerating very dysfunctional and disrespectful behavior from his various female partners. The way he gives up his own needs and yields to their demands. Yet this man is very powerful in the rest of his life. So there is no RATIONAL explanation for his behavior with his women. In my mind, that means the explanation lies in some type of childhood wounding, even if we haven't identified the specific chain of causality.

But you don't NEED to identify specific events. You need only accept that something beyond the rational and cognitive may be lodged in your psyche and amplifying your perception of threat. It can cause you to react to present-day events, in which you are in no actual danger, with reactive anxiety (subtle to intense) that interferes with your groundedness and Masculine core.

And this dynamic, which started with your "all-powerful" parents, will often expand to include a broader range of people in your **adult** life. It will most visibly manifest with "authority" figures in your life who have some type of power — organizational power, financial power, physical power or size, social power, the power of attractiveness, or an assertive personality. Women specifically may hold the power of attractiveness, the power of her approval, the power of sex, and the inherent biological power of the Feminine over you.

Others' power makes them important to you. So the prospect of these people disapproving of and rejecting you in some way, and then "leaving you" as a result, would be very painful. For many men, it can be a beautiful woman, your own woman, a socially dominant acquaintance, someone you've just met, or a higher-up at work. **All of these are people with power, and so you're reluctant to disappoint them.** For whatever reason, their opinion matters to you (even if you pretend it doesn't) and disappointing them threatens your sense of belonging (straight out of Maslow's hierarchy).

This is the "threat" that we've been discussing. Because **not meeting the expectations of others carries the potential for loss of something important**: the other person's love, their regard for your competence, their attention, their attraction to you, their opinion of you, your self-esteem, your time, your money, your career advancement, etc. These things are important to you. You don't want to lose them, and your childhood wounding amplifies both the risk and magnitude of that happening. And thus you go into a threat state and feel anxiety.

More often than not this is subtle rather than dramatic. It quietly impacts your way of being, often manifesting in the non-Masculine behaviors we've discussed.

Many men spend their lives avoiding disappointing others. None of us are immune, including me. I remember once having a boss whom I respected and liked immensely. He liked me too. I was not a sycophant by any means, but at some point, I realized that I didn't always speak my full truth with him because I didn't want to rock the boat with our relationship. I had to go through my own inner process of getting OK with disappointing him someday. And that is the problem — **because of your fear of disappointing others, you begin to subconsciously operate in ways that you think will avoid this outcome.**

THREAT DISTORTS REALITY

Threat is a powerful phenomenon that can radically shift your entire physiology and perceptions. When you become triggered because of a fear of disapproval or abandonment, anxiety kicks in and usually causes muscle clenching, constricted breathing, diminished awareness, and compromised cognitive activity. You're not as smart, creative, or witty as you normally are. Emotional and cognitive capabilities are diminished as you go on auto-pilot to respond to the "threat" your body-mind perceives. You don't process what others are saying quite as clearly. Everything seems a little more dangerous. You are no longer quite as present in this moment.

Imagine a time when you got a little tongue-tied meeting a beautiful woman. That is exactly what I'm talking about. And when you said something awkward, it got worse. Sound familiar? You were experiencing a sense of threat.

Let me be clear that I'm not talking about overt panic attacks here. Rather, the anxiety usually operates in the background, subtly influencing your behavior. It is akin to someone who is lying — you may

not be able to tell with your eyes and ears, but a lie detector can pic
their inner turmoil. This anxiety is the same — you may seem normal,
able to operate and carry on a conversation, but you're not operating
out of full choice nor fully in the present moment.

**Anxiety is like radio static played on full-blast, but instead of block-
ing out sound, it's purpose is to block out the emotions you don't
want to feel**: primarily fear, but secondarily shame, anger, or sadness.
The body-mind blocks out what it doesn't want to experience.

Yet rarely do these emotions signal any ACTUAL threat to you. You
need only do what I think of as a Reality Test: look up at the sun in
the blue sky, look around at the birds and trees and flowers, or think
of the great things in your life. You'll realize instantly that you are fine.
You are safe. Nothing can really hurt you. And yet the threat and anxiety push you into Approval Seeking Behavior: trying a little too hard
in a conversation in order to make someone like you, holding back
your true opinions to avoid displeasing others, etc. As long as you are
dealing with someone who is important to you, who has some form
of power in this world, the potential for it exists. And, again, we're not
talking about a reaction in which you're sweating and shaking, but
rather one in which **your mind is self-correcting in all kinds of little
ways to gain approval or avoid rejection**. You may not notice it, but
others will feel it. Particularly the sensitive woman in your life.

Threat and anxiety are not something that OTHER people experience, the weak and nervous ones. These are body-mind phenomena
that we ALL experience, often every day, in mild to acute ways. This
includes you.

By far, **your most effective path to growing into your Masculine power** is to train your nervous system to handle the intensity that accompanies threat and anxiety. This is your path to freedom.

DYSFUNCTIONAL ANXIETY STRATEGIES

There are five other dysfunctional strategies that men often employ. They include:

1. Contraction (including withdrawal, shame, hiding)
2. Collapse
3. Defense (defending, explaining, lying)
4. Distraction
5. Blame

Let's look at each of these individually.

Contraction is when you either energetically or physically "disappear". Energetic disappearance generally occurs when you feel hurt or shame and don't want to be "seen". It is characterized by introversion or non-engagement: lack of eye contact, lack of verbalization, and an absence of assertiveness. Energetically, you become very small, as if you are a little boy hiding. Let's say you have a colossal fight with your woman, one that feels intractable. In a state of contraction, you might storm out of the conversation and then give her the cold shoulder afterward. Instead of staying in the fire and engaged, you are withdrawing and using the silent treatment to get her to change her behavior. But this is not you holding space, staying grounded, or creating structure and safety for her.

Collapse refers to you acting sad and helpless in response to another's displeasure, appealing to their pity. It could sound like "*I can't ever get anything right with you.*" It is you playing the victim. Or, you simply give in to the others' opinions or demands, essentially letting them control you: "*Fine. Whatever you want.*" This is your body-mind just entirely giving up and playing the role of victim, rather than being in touch with your needs and standing your ground in asking for them. You are reacting rather than responding.

Defense is when you get defensive in the face of your woman criticizing or blaming you for something. You are trying to explain your innocent motivations, or otherwise convince her that she shouldn't feel the way she is feeling. If only you could "correct the facts" in her mind, she'd magically stop being mad at you. Her "disapproval" would change to "approval". Too bad it never works that way. We'll discuss this in depth in Chapter 14.

Distraction is what you do, consciously or unconsciously, to avoid or bleed off the excess energy of anxiety. Losing yourself in alcohol, work, or porn are common methods. In the moment, it could be you talking too much or too fast, moving your body nervously, tapping your foot, or anxiously checking your phone. All of these things distract you and help you avoid having to feel your own anxiety, anger, shame, or disappointment.

Blame is your attempt to avoid being "wrong" or "bad" by pointing out the culpability of the other person. It is a form of defensiveness that involves counterattacking the other. If you can make them wrong, that means you must be "right", and thus their "disapproval" would turn to "approval". Or you can simply feel that you have the high moral ground and thus can ignore their point of view. You are taking the energy of the anxiety that you feel and redirecting it back at the other person in order to avoid having to deal with it.

Each of these five categories of behavior serves to help you avoid feeling your anxiety, to turn perceived disapproval into approval, or to avoid or deflect negative attention. But none of them support others' perception of your Masculine power nor create more connection and trust with those around you.

Now, let's look back at a few of the non-Masculine behaviors from the list in Chapter 5 and see if we can map these strategies onto them:

- **Get defensive when verbally attacked**. Method: *Defense*. Being verbally attacked means you've angered someone and risk their disapproval. It is certainly an anxiety-creating occurrence. In an effort to stop the feeling of anxiety, you go into Defense and seek to "correct the facts" in the other person's mind through explaining or blaming. Rather than allowing your nervous system to tolerate the anxiety and empathizing with the others' point of view, you seek to make it all stop.

- **Become passive around Feminine energy or dominant male energy**. Method: *Collapse and Approval Seeking*. Feminine females and dominant males often both possess enormous perceived power. You may naturally fear disappointing or displeasing them. So you do nothing that might elicit their disapproval. You may become cautious or passive, and give up your own desires to satisfy their real or imagined needs.

- **Withdraw when feeling hurt**. Method: *Contraction*. Whether through an uncomfortable truth, malicious insult, or careless comment, the other person triggers shame in you. Anxiety arises, and you're unable to just sit with the emotion and share the "ouch" with the other person. So you storm out or give the other person the cold shoulder.

- **Nervously fidget or tap hands or feet**. Method: *Distraction*. These types of repetitive movements are simply the body-mind's way of unconsciously bleeding off the energy of anxiety when your nervous system doesn't have the capacity to handle it.
- **Attack back when being shamed**. Method: *Blame*. You'll do anything to avoid the pain of shame. You blow up in anger at the other person as a way to gain the upper hand and make the feeling stop.
- **Ramble on to fill awkward silences**. Method: *Distraction and Seeking Approval*. This happens with uncomfortable silences in conversation. You might interpret a gap in the flow as an indication that they're bored with talking to you and are disengaging. Anxiety arises as a result, so you talk to distract yourself from it, or to rekindle the conversation and in order to generate a signal of approval.
- **Try to initiate sex indirectly rather than directly**. Method: *Contraction and Seeking Approval*. You don't assert your sexual desire. Rather, you make small tentative bids, afraid to truly own your sexuality. This is different than being sensitive to your partner or observing the rules of consent — rather, it has the energy of begging for sex rather than powerfully leading your woman into her sexuality.
- **Act like a "nice guy" or try to please others**. Method: *Collapse and Seeking Approval*. This is the classic case of you being nice and accommodating, eschewing your own preferences in order to seem non-threatening and to avoid the other person's displeasure.
- **Slouch while standing or sitting**. Method: *Contraction*. This is, of course, an unconscious behavior — no one would choose to slouch. But conventional wisdom says it is the body-mind trying to "become invisible" by literally closing in on itself and becom-

ing smaller. It is your unconscious way of not attracting anxiety-producing attention from others.

- **Move and speak rapidly**. Method: *Distraction*. A man in his power moves and talks deliberately and consciously. But the ungrounded man often has rapid movements and speech, not unlike how a bird moves its body. This is how you bleed off the energy of anxiety.
- **Deny that he's feeling angry or scared**. Method: *Seeking Approval*. You are afraid of confronting others, so you deny your anger. Or, you feel shame around your fear, so you deny it so that you don't look weak.

These categories aren't intended to be 100 percent distinct from one another. They overlap. But I hope they provide enough structure to help you better interpret the underlying causes of some non-Masculine behaviors. And that they shed light on the role that threat and anxiety play in each.

CONCLUSION

Threat and anxiety are phenomena that will distort your reality and sap you of your Masculine power. But there are things you can do to combat them, and we'll spend the bulk of Chapters 9 and 10 on this topic. Whether it is through reframing your perceptions or daily embodiment practice, you **can** affect this situation.

It will be a long road — these things don't change quickly. But it will be worth it. Your entire reality will shift. Circumstances that used to seem intense and anxiety-provoking will magically no longer be a big deal. You'll come to realize that it was all in your head.

CHAPTER 9

EMOTIONS

In this chapter, we examine a topic that has forever baffled men: our emotions. Get to know them or you will be run by them rather than operating out of choice. Your tendency will be to suppress them. Their energy will build up in your system and leak out as anxiety, which only makes you even more reactive. Even worse, when your woman inevitably senses you hiding or avoiding your emotions, she will feel less connected to you and, therefore, more closed to you.

Don't get caught in the trap of thinking that processing and expressing your emotions means you're weak. On the contrary, it makes you stronger in your woman's eyes and more robust to intensity. Denying or being run by them is what makes you seem weak.

AN OVERVIEW OF EMOTION

I start by posing the question: *What exactly is an emotion?* Although emotions are unimaginably complex, I like to think of them very simply: they are the body-mind's way of automating a set of thoughts and physical reactions that allow you to efficiently interact with the world. You can act without having to think through each step.

In the case of some of the darker emotions like fear or anger, they are designed to protect you from threat. The body-mind has a very efficient learning system. When something threatens you, the body-mind quickly learns how to avoid that same experience in the future.

If the threat is physical, your eyes and ears sense signals that resemble prior threats, the heart starts pushing blood faster, the muscles tense in anticipation, the eyes become wider to take in more visual input, and the brain blocks out extraneous information and focuses your attention on your immediate environment. All of these activities and reactions are packaged up in the emotion called fear. You don't have to think about any of this. It just happens without the brain having to process it all in real-time.

The mechanism is not perfect. Your mind becomes hypervigilant for signals of threat. If the original experience was traumatic enough, the "vigilance dial" is now probably turned up to the point of overreacting to input and seeing threats that aren't necessarily there. But the body-mind is very serious about protecting you, so it uses a "better safe than sorry" approach.

The hypervigilance works great to keep you alive in the face of physical threats. But for emotional situations, it can cause some dysfunction. It can cause you to be overly reactive to certain emotions that arise, even when there is no real "threat" to you. Keep this in mind as we dive into the emotions below. It is your overreaction to these automated emotional responses that often creates so much anxiety within you and takes you out of the present moment. **If you understand your emotions and are not ruled by them, you will naturally be less reactive and more grounded.**

Below we will take a look at four primary emotions: fear, shame, sadness, and anger (I won't cover the lighter emotions of joy and love here). Note that I am not presuming to give the definitive definition of each emotion. There is an entire field of psychology to deal with that. Rather, I am offering my own lens on them, one that is intended to make them more actionable in the context of this book's theme of living from your Masculine core.

FEAR

We start with fear because I believe it lies underneath all of the other negative emotions. In my experience, shame, anger, and sadness all tie back to some type of fear.

We all know fear well — the terror, the desire to hide, the anxiety that arises in the body, the overwhelming desire to avoid a certain outcome. It's a complicated mix of stimuli, old wounds, and real or imagined danger. So let's try to break it down a bit in order to make it more actionable.

For purposes of discussion, I like to frame all of the automatic physical reactions — wide eyes, sweating, clenching, hyper-focused mind, etc. — under the umbrella of anxiety. Let's separate them from the fear itself in this examination.

Now, let's try to define the fear itself. My actionable definition of fear is this: **the mind's resistance to an outcome that it doesn't want to happen**. Why does it resist? Because traumatic past experiences have lodged themselves into your psyche, and your subconscious now considers similar outcomes in the present day to be absolutely "unacceptable". The mind vigorously resists such outcomes by putting you into a threat state that either paralyzes you from taking action, or creates massive amounts of anxiety that block out your full awareness of the present moment — like radio static turned up to a high volume that blocks out your ability to hear other sounds. It seems that the subconscious is naive enough to think that if you block out the awareness of something, you can block out the thing itself (the outcome being resisted). Sadly, that's not how things work. That outcome may still happen, and the circumstances still exist.

The opposite of fear would be surrender. You no longer resist the possibility of the outcome happening. You accept it. You may not like it, and you may suffer because of it. But you accept that it <u>could</u> happen and that you will survive it if it does.

I agree this is an unconventional definition, so let me illustrate with a few examples:

- A man cuts into a long line of people waiting at the ATM outside your bank. You consider saying something, but feel fear of a physical confrontation. This is your subconscious mind resisting the possibility of this outcome because it deems a physical confrontation as both likely and absolutely unacceptable.
- Your girlfriend has done something to make you very angry. You would like to set a hard boundary, but are afraid that she'll have an intensely negative reaction. Your mind has not reconciled itself to this happening, so it resists doing anything that might cause that outcome.
- You've dreamed of starting your own business, but you fear that quitting your job would wreck your financial situation. Again, the fear is your mind resisting this outcome because of a subconscious belief that you could not recover financially from a temporary loss of income.

- A single man sees a beautiful woman at a party and would like to approach her. But he fears her rejection. This is his mind resisting this outcome because it deems the possibility of rejection to be so painful that it cannot be allowed to happen.

In each case, the subconscious mind has classified these outcomes as unacceptable, almost to the point of being "unsurvivable", so to speak. Yet **most fears arise unexamined and may be somewhat irrational**. Many are born of overreaction to signals that resemble those from prior traumatic experiences. Someone who was exposed to violence in his family at a young age may overreact to the potential of violence from a guy in an ATM line. Someone with abandonment issues may overreact to the possibility of his girlfriend leaving him out of anger. The overreactions lead the mind to classify all kinds of outcomes as "unacceptable" even though they may not actually be likely or catastrophic.

So, the subconscious resists these outcomes and uses anxiety to guide your behavior so they don't happen. **You begin to live life cautiously and anxiously in order to avoid your fears**.

Overcoming fear means challenging your subconscious about the outcome being "unacceptable". In that context, I offer you a straightforward path to dealing with fear: **the key to overcoming your fears is simply to accept that what you fear <u>could</u> happen, and if it does you will still be fine.** Surrender to the possibility. This doesn't mean that you roll over and let it happen, or that you assume it <u>will</u> happen. Rather, you simply accept that everything will be OK if it does happen, even while you still prefer that it does not.

Sit down and close your eyes right now. Imagine the guy cutting in the ATM line. Imagine yourself saying something to him. Feel your mind's resistance to the outcome of him confronting you, and relax into it. Even if he took a swing at you, know that it would hurt a bit but you'd be fine. Come to accept that a confrontation <u>could</u> happen and that you'll be fine if it does.

This is the mental exercise you must run over and over to train your mind out of its own limiting patterns. It is akin to visualization exercises that professional athletes do. Repeatedly envisioning yourself doing something convinces the mind that you can do this thing.

Imagine another situation, that of sharing your truth with your girlfriend. Feel your mind's resistance to the possibility that she'll blow up at you. Surrender to it. It will be painful, but you will be fine. Even in the unlikely event that she was to break up with you, see yourself questioning the rightness of a relationship with such a reactive woman. It is not the end of the world. You'll survive.

Picture yourself quitting your job to start the business of your dreams. Envision the worst-case scenario that it fails within six months. Ask yourself, is there any reason I just can't go get another job? You may have lost tens of thousands of dollars, but the remainder of your savings may be enough for your retirement. Again, it is not the end of the world.

If you're single, imagine approaching that beautiful woman and having her response be *"I don't talk to losers."* Remind yourself that rejection by this beautiful creature doesn't define you in any way, that it is more about her state of mind than your desirability. Her response means nothing and nothing has changed. So relax your mind's resistance to this outcome.

In each case, you're coming to grips with the fact that the worst-case consequences of each action are perfectly survivable, despite your subconscious beliefs. And in that knowledge, you can allow your body-mind to accept the potential for them to happen. You don't have to like the outcome. You just have to **develop the core belief that you'll be fine if it does happen**. In that acceptance, you will see the fear start to fade. And this is the crux of why I define fear in this way. Once you surrender to these "dire" outcomes, the fear abates.

Of course, this is much easier said than done. You will not achieve this capability just by reading this book. You are going to have to train your nervous system through practice over many years. One of the ways I recommend doing this is to use *Provocation Meditation* (see Chapter 10). Sit, close your eyes, and seek to identify a few of your current fears. Then keep asking yourself "*What if that happens?*" over and over so that you can envision the entire chain of events. Then sit with that outcome and use the techniques I've shared to make friends with that potential reality.

Feel the fear in you arise as anxiety in the body. Feel the clenching of your jaw and other muscles. Relax into it. Feel your constricted breathing. Relax into it. Find your inner smile while still envisioning the outcome. Then open your eyes and do a Reality Test. Notice the sun still shining and the birds still singing, even while you envision the outcome happening. Use all of this to come to a KNOWING that you WILL be OK, even if this event occurs. You may still seek to avoid it, but only up to the point where it does not prevent you from living your life fully or being the man you want to be.

SADNESS

I see sadness as **resistance to loss**. It is the non-acceptance of something that is now gone from or exiting your life. Examples could include:

- A close friend or family member dies.
- Your woman breaks up with you.
- A close friend moves to another state.
- Someone close to you betrays you.
- You begin to notice the loss of your health and capability.
- You move away and are no longer part of a community you once enjoyed.
- Your physical environment is being negatively affected by pollution or other human development.
- You lose a job.

Sadness arises because of the gap between current reality and a past reality that you can't quite let go of. The more important the loss, the more tightly will you grasp on to a past reality and the greater the magnitude and duration of your pain. Of course, your conscious mind probably knows the loss is real and irreversible, but the subconscious does not want to let go.

This is natural, and it is very healthy to allow sadness the time it needs to arise and flow through you. You don't need to rush the unfolding. It will take as long as it takes. But you can support yourself by finding the places in you that are resisting reality. Relax into and accept what is actually happening.

Absent a natural progression toward acceptance of the new reality, sadness turns into depression. This is a state in which everything seems bleak and hopeless. Your energy for career, intimate, and social endeavors can be sapped. I myself had a taste of depression after the end of my marriage. It was very challenging for me to accept circumstances as they were, and what had been lost — my family unit, companionship, and trust in someone I never thought would falter. The duration and intensity of my sadness were prolonged by not fully accepting my new reality.

If you find yourself in a depressed state, don't hesitate to get professional help. But while you do this, I encourage you to put your attention on this notion of acceptance. Using your pain like a trail of breadcrumbs, trace your thoughts and emotions back to the truths you are not accepting. The job is gone. Your female partner is gone. A relative is gone. Your trust in a person is gone. And these realities are not likely to change. **You suffer not because of reality itself, but because you resist reality**.

A client of mine went through a painful period where his resistance to his own reality caused him months of self-imposed isolation:

> *Chad's girlfriend of four years had broken up with him. He was devastated because he had thought that they were very compatible. Six months afterward, he still expressed sadness to me about it. By itself, this seemed natural. But he hadn't been on a second date in all that time, and he admitted that his energy was a bit low and it probably showed on these dates. More importantly, I still sensed a "Why? Why!?" element to his inner narrative.*

I shared with him how palpably his impotent non-acceptance was manifesting in him. It was clearly affecting his dating life. It wasn't for me to judge whether his healing was progressing "fast enough". But it was my role to point out how his non-acceptance of reality was still gripping him. His ex-girlfriend was irreversibly gone from his life, and there were absolutely no signs of that changing. The constricted way he was showing up in his life was him operating not out of choice, but rather out of the pain and resistance he was experiencing. He was reacting, not responding, to the circumstances in which he found himself.

SHAME

Shame is anathema to Masculine leadership. A leader is visible and energetically big. In contrast, a person engulfed in shame simply wants to shrink, disappear, and not be seen by anyone. Put simply, **shame is the fear of having your undesirable traits seen by others**. You might feel ashamed of your height, looks, intelligence, imperfect skin, the sound of your voice, or how much money you make. You could be feeling shame about something you've said or done, such as yelling at your kids. Shame lies to you and tells you that if others were to know these things about you they would see your unworthiness and therefore reject or abandon you.

If left unchecked, this feeling can metastasize into toxic shame, which is the belief that **you are holistically and fundamentally flawed**. John Bradshaw describes it very well in *Healing the Shame that Binds You*:

> *The feeling of shame has the same demonic potential to encompass our whole personality. Instead of the momentary feeling of being limited, making a mistake, littleness, or being less attractive or talented than someone else, a person can come to believe that his whole self is fundamentally flawed and defective. Healthy guilt would say "I made a mistake or a blunder, and I can repair that blunder." Unhealthy shame has a person say "I am a mistake — everything I do is flawed and defective."*

Shame causes you to believe that you ARE bad, rather than you DID something bad. It is common for this to play out when your woman is mad at you, as in this example with a client:

> *Jake shared that he is so busy at work that he will often procrastinate on home maintenance. At one point the plumbing had been acting up and two toilets were getting clogged. He applied some liquid clog remover and it helped a bit, just enough to get the toilets functional. But a week later, one of them clogged again and made a mess. His wife was livid that he hadn't taken care of it fully the first time. She said to him that night, "Why do I have to be the man and call the plumber?" This made him angry and was the start of a big fight.*

Jake may have been feeling anger, but underneath he was feeling ashamed that he hadn't handled things. He held a belief (as did she, apparently) that the man of the house takes care of physical home maintenance, even if that just means calling a plumber. Her cutting remarks challenged his self-image of being a man who handles things. His embarrassment at not having gotten the plumbing fixed bloomed into a shame response based on a subconscious belief that it meant he was not, in fact, a "real man". Which then created fear that his wife saw him this way and would thus be less attracted to him and vulnerable to another man's attention. He believed he was flawed and inferred that women leave flawed men. Of course, he covered all of this up with anger directed at her. Naturally, it spiraled out of control quickly between the two of them.

His shame response prevented him from seeing what was actually going on for her (which we discovered later when he asked her): she was feeling that her well-being (as represented by a functioning house) wasn't top of mind for him because work was a higher priority. For her, this represented a lack of love on his part and thus a break in their connection, which made her feel unsafe. Although her approach was clumsy and toxic, the truth was that **her reaction came not out of a rejection of him but rather out of her desire to feel taken care of and loved by him**.

The pain of not feeling loved and cared for by you is so intense to your woman that it can cause her to react toxically. She'll react out of her own wounded places, which probably include past experiences with you but also many that predate you. In this state, she'll wield shame as a weapon.

This is the part that we men chronically misunderstand. She's angry about what you DID and is reacting out of a desire to feel closer to you. Unfortunately, if you suffer from toxic shame, you might think she's criticizing your whole being and essentially judging and rejecting you. You're globalizing her comments.

This will feel like she's questioning your basic worthiness. You may then react from your own wounded places and go into a shame response. Her words may touch a nerve connected to something deep down you'd rather hide — your insecurities, failures, fears, the fact that you don't make as much money as the guy next door, that time you screwed up at work. You live in fear of her (or anyone) discovering these things that you would hide.

The psyche has many different methods to cope with shame:

- *You tell little lies.* It could be minor omissions of fact or outright untruths. You tell these to others, but eventually you start believing them yourself. You create what's known as a "false self", which is an airtight self-image that does not include your "flaws". It is the man with the unsophisticated upbringing who claims to love wine in order to sound sophisticated instead of just saying *"You know, I never developed a taste for it."* Or the man who falsely claims to not be hurt by some criticism he received. You hide the "real you" behind this false self. Unfortunately, this precludes the possibility of true honesty and authenticity in your relationships. And you'll always know you're living a lie.

- *You may simply disappear*, meaning that you stay quiet or withdraw, avoiding interactions that might expose the "you" that you try to hide. Your subconscious lives by the motto "Better to remain silent and be thought a fool than to speak and remove all doubt." This characterizes it well because the shame-based individual lives in fear that he'll show a part of himself that will make others dislike him. Ironically, it is your withdrawal that actually turns others off. You are so afraid of the possibility of "removing all doubt" that you create a certainty out of the "thought a fool" part. All because of your shame.

- *You live out of a belief in your own inferiority*. And despite your efforts, you won't be able to hide it over the long term. It will leak out in your energy and interactions with others. It becomes a self-fulfilling prophecy — if you feel this way about yourself, others will pick up on it and feel that way about you as well.

- *You give up your needs*. Your shame causes you to believe that you're not worthy enough to have needs or impose them on others. So you won't demand what you're due and you won't ask for what you want.

- *You become a "nice guy"*. There is a great book on how men put on a persona of being nice, harmless, and needless in order not to upset or inconvenience anyone around them. If they can hide their mistakes and emotions, they believe that they'll become what others want them to be.

- *You display addictive behavior.* You use your addictions in order to numb the pain of feeling your shame. Drugs, alcohol, porn, web surfing, social media, and video games are the vices of choice for many men looking to escape from the gnawing feeling of their toxic shame.

These are all examples of you shrinking in the world rather than becoming bigger and stepping into your role as a Masculine leader. If you're caught in the cycle of shame you'll tend to not speak firmly and clearly, assert yourself, or have strong eye contact or posture, all necessary elements of a strong Masculine presence.

You will find that the amount of shame, and the compensatory behaviors above, will vary with the importance of the other person. Someone who is not important to you likely cannot induce shame in you. No matter what your neighbor's seven-year-old child says to you, he probably won't be able to make you feel ashamed. But if you're interacting with a successful acquaintance or a dominant colleague at work, the stakes go up and the propensity for a shame response in certain circumstances goes up. If it's a beautiful woman or your angry woman, the potential for toxic shame gets even higher. This is because those with power and authority are important to us, and we care what they think of us. So **your subconscious wants to hide your "flawed" parts from them at all costs**.

So, how does a man overcome his own shame? The answer is surprisingly simple, although hard to do: **come out of hiding.** Shame thrives in the dark and cannot stand the logical scrutiny of light. So **start to surface the things about which you hold shame**.

Years ago, when my marriage had ended and my then-wife had taken a new lover, I was an emotional mess. I did an exercise to help clear some of my shame. I camped by myself for two days and used the time for soul-searching and creation of a list of five things which I wouldn't want to admit to the world. One of these things was a fear that "*This man was a better lover than me.*" I didn't know if that was true, but it was a story and a fear that preyed on my insecurity in that raw time of my life. It was actually hard to even acknowledge that story to myself because it painfully challenged what my ego so desperately wanted to believe about myself — that I was a man who could uniquely satisfy his woman. The ego doesn't like its self-images shattered. But as painful as this process was, it was a powerful aid in helping me let go of the shame and anxiety I felt around it.

With my list in hand, I did many hours of *Provocation Meditation* (see Chapter 10) on each item. I came into contact with the vulnerable part of myself which resisted each of them. I acclimated myself to the feelings of shame, fear, and anxiety that they created in me. And then practiced accepting and owning these feelings.

Later, I then did something quite difficult: I read the list to someone close to me with whom I felt safe. Just the act of revealing these things which I would keep hidden was incredibly liberating.

And the first step in this process was a commitment to being fully honest with <u>myself</u>. We spend a lifetime hiding things from others, so much so that we begin to even fool ourselves.

To surrender into the reality of your shame and let it go is a huge weight off your shoulders. You lay down the burden of having to hide or defend.

As you take this newfound openness out into the world with others, let your orientation be "*Yea, I have this thing about me I'm not proud of. Big deal.*" Surrender into it. Unabashedly own up to your points of shame. You may not like them, but you're no longer trying to conceal them.

ANGER

Anger is the most confusing of emotions for men. Society sends conflicting messages. Express too much anger, and you're a misogynistic bully. Too little, and you're a doormat. The net effect is that you either blast others irresponsibly with anger (often to cover up other emotions) or suppress your anger and forgo your own needs in order to avoid confrontation. Few are skilled at expressing anger while remaining in connection with others and with their own needs.

The way you deal with anger is often not out of conscious choice, but rather silently guided by your childhood experiences. If Mom or Dad was physically or verbally violent with you when he or she was angry, then your psyche may strive to "never be like that", or might unconsciously recreate it. If anger was implicitly forbidden in your house, then your psyche may have absorbed that anger is not acceptable. Without consciously choosing, you're just playing out a script from your past and either suppressing or irresponsibly blasting out anger.

Let's take a closer look and try to demystify this emotion. To me, **the simplest essence of anger is that it is a signal that something important to you is being threatened**. That "something" could be a resource like time, possessions, or money. It may be the physical and emotional safety of you or those you care about. Or, it could be part of your self-identity being threatened, which happens when someone else's actions or words contradict the image you have of yourself (i.e., when your feelings are hurt).

Let's illustrate all of these through some examples:

- You're angry at your child who won't listen to your repeated requests to pick up his room. This is a drain on your precious time and attention because you're repeatedly having to check up on the child and repeat the request. It also threatens the subconscious notion you hold that you have the power to control the actions of your family members. If they disobey, it might suggest that you don't necessarily have that power.

- Your wife criticizes your fiscal responsibility in front of friends and you're angry. This might threaten a principle you hold that you and your wife are loyal to each other first and foremost. If she couldn't be more discreet with her criticism here, your mind naturally spins out in fear that she is capable of being disloyal in other, more significant ways. You thought she had your back but her words threaten that belief. And, at a deeper level, there was probably a kernel of truth in her complaint, and it threatened the self-image you hold that you're a man who is responsible with money.

- You're livid that a driver aggressively cut in front of you while you're driving your family across town. This very obviously threatens the safety of your family. And, at a deeper level, it feels like blatant disrespect by the other driver and threatens your sense that you are worthy of respect from others.

When you encounter these threats to what's important to you, something is activated inside you. It feels like a rumble and a fire within. The healthy man sees it as a signal to wake up, pay attention, and try to see what important thing is being threatened, or what boundary has been crossed.

Anger is a tremendous ally for you if you understand why it's arising. It tells you what is meaningful. Embrace it. Its intensity can instantly grab your attention. And the energy it creates in your body can quickly propel you into decisive action to protect what's important. Viewed through this lens, you can see that anger is one of the most important emotions for a man to know and harness.

But anger can take a more toxic form, where it comes up reactively in response to feelings of shame, fear, and hurt. In these cases, anger is an unconscious protection mechanism that numbs out these feelings inside you and draws attention to others and <u>their</u> transgressions. You are angry AT them, and the solution to the entire situation is that THEY need to change or fix something. As long as you are focused on them, you don't have to feel your own shame, anxiety, fear, or hurt because it is THEIR fault. So, **reactive anger often manifests as blame that your subconscious uses to avoid deeper emotions**.

One of my clients shared with me an episode that illustrates this dynamic well:

> *Blake's wife Jessica was upset that the laundry room was so tiny that it was difficult to do the laundry. There was little space for multiple baskets, and no room to lay out clothes to air dry. One day in frustration, she vented rhetorically: "Why can't we afford a bigger house!" Blake took*

this as a criticism of him, a reference to the fact that he didn't make enough money to support them buying a larger home. It was something around which he'd had some long-standing shame, which was converted to anger directed at her: "What is your problem? Why do you have to be such a bitch all of the time? You're never satisfied!" Even though she had not given any overt indication she thought he didn't make enough money, he went into full reaction mode as if she had. His subconscious was running the show and used anger and blame to protect him from having to acknowledge and feel his own shame.

Now, even worse than reactive anger is repressed anger. Most guys have a hard time expressing their anger, so they go into denial about it. They claim not to be angry at all, but then withdraw or become passive-aggressive. Neither is the mark of a powerful man leading others to more openness. My client Jordan shared this story with me:

Jordan shared with me that his wife had recently had an "emotional affair" with another man and had admitted it in their couple's therapy session that week. One morning at the house by himself, in a fit of pain, fear, and rage, he lashed out and punched the wall, leaving a gaping hole. Later that night, his wife returned and saw the hole. During their now nightly fights, she yelled: "Why can't you just tell me you're angry instead of destroying the house?" His response was "I'm not angry. I just lost control for a second."

I just stared at him for a good ten seconds, trying to absorb the irony of his story. In all of my experience, this was the penultimate example of someone suppressing anger. I cannot think of a more appropriate scenario for a man to be angry and to be justified in saying so. Jordan's wife had crossed a clear boundary. Her actions threatened the existence of the relationship, and that relationship was very important to Jordan. Yet he was unable to acknowledge his own anger.

This is one of the great mysteries for men, how it is so hard for them to just say "*I'm angry.*" But to me, it is clear that this tendency usually stems from one's childhood. If anger was abundant in your life growing up, it may have been scary enough to your childhood self that you shut down the ability to ever be angry. If anger was not allowed in your childhood home, then possibly you cut off that part of you. So when anger is scary or unacceptable, you convert it into more acceptable feelings. John Bradshaw sheds light on this in his book *Healing The Shame that Binds You*:

> *Anger is often blocked from conscious awareness and converted into more tolerable or family-authorized feelings, such as hurt or guilt. The person feeling the anger no longer feels it; he feels the acceptable feeling.*

Your family norms may have made it unsafe to feel or express anger. So you suppressed it or converted it into something more acceptable.

In effect, this childhood dynamic saps your adult self of confidence around the validity of your anger and the boundary that has been crossed. You begin to question whether you are justified in being angry and expressing it, particularly if the other person is an authority figure or otherwise very important to you. It is this dynamic that often has men holding back their anger.

Unskillful handling of your anger will disrupt connection with others. When it builds up and explodes as aggression, it will make your woman feel unsafe. On the flip side, if you suppress it, she won't be able to feel you.

But it does not need to be this way. You can step up to take charge of your anger and actually **convert it into something that draws you and your woman closer**.

First, rather than suppress, **welcome the anger in with gratitude that it is giving you a powerful reminder of what's important to you**. Jordan could have done this. That hole in the wall was a clear sign of how important his wife was to him. Of how scared her emotional infidelity made him. And of how strongly he felt that infidelity is NOT acceptable. Anger would have made him instantly crystal clear on his love, fear, and boundaries.

Anger is clarifying. A man with clarity is powerful. So, **when you feel angry, welcome it and ask yourself what it is making clear for you**. Notice the anger in the moment, and trace it back to the source. Anger almost ALWAYS covers up an underlying fear and a need. The fear relates to something important that is being threatened. Anger is the subconscious mind's protection against that fear. The underlying need is what you want from your woman or the world in order to feel safe. Allow your attention to move past the anger itself toward the fear and need underneath.

Once you do this, wholeheartedly accept what you find. And then **share the anger, the fear, and the need with your partner**. Sharing the anger conveys the intensity and seriousness. Sharing the fear reveals the truth of what's happening for you. Sharing the need gives her an opportunity to better meet you as a partner. You'll be shocked by how this kind of vulnerable sharing will open your woman up and make her responsive to your needs in a way that blaming her would not.

Your second step is to **allow the energy of anger to spur you into action**. Convert it into motivation to protect what is important. Jordan could have used his anger as motivation to turn his new self-awareness into action: to powerfully declare his love for his wife, vulnerably share his fear and hurt, and to set a non-negotiable boundary around fidelity. Anger exists to galvanize and focus you and spur you into action to protect what's important. Use it, and don't be afraid of it. You can feel and accept the savagery of anger within you without being a savage. The intensity of the savagery is only an indication of how much you care about the issue.

The most effective action you can take is to express. It can sound like: "I'm angry about _____ because _____ is so important to me. What I need from you is _____." At the same time, be sure to do a few things:

- Maintain eye contact with the other person.
- Stay present and in connection to them.
- Be in touch with your own heart and your care for this person.
- Acknowledge your underlying feelings of fear and longing rather than just the anger.
- Above all, remember that you have a right to your anger and the underlying need.
- Stay present for their response rather than "fire and forget".

In Jordan's case, it might have looked like the following: "*Baby, I am deeply angry with you because of what's been happening with this other man. You are very important to me and this whole thing has shaken me to my core. I want us to be together but now I feel so emotionally unsafe. I know I cannot stay in a relationship with a person who can't hold a strong container of fidelity. Does this make sense?"* Jordan is clearly expressing his anger, fear, needs, and boundaries while staying in connection with his wife.

You can express all of this with quiet intensity or with a raised voice, fire in your eyes, and a shaking fist. Both approaches are fine. As long as you're staying in connection with the other person, owning the anger rather than just blaming, and vulnerably revealing your underlying need.

Absent your ability to express anger, you won't be able to set boundaries. You will actually be training people to disregard your needs, to walk right past your unspoken boundaries without consideration.

You cannot provide Masculine leadership without a deep relationship to your own anger.

KNOWING YOUR EMOTIONS

Masculine leadership requires you to know your own emotions. If you don't, they will control you. Your suppression of them will prevent real connection with your woman. Your denial of them makes you look weak in her eyes.

Sadly, few men are emotionally aware. Most are openly dismissive of emotionality and are stubborn about it. You mock and avoid this thing known as "getting in touch with your feelings". You joke about it with your friends and label it as something that women do. You wear your lack of emotion like a badge of honor.

Let me correct this misconception: **knowing your emotions is absolutely central to being Masculine**. Why? Because many of the fights or points of tension with your woman occur because she does not feel emotionally close to you. A high-quality woman will not feel connected to a chronically emotionally closed man. No matter how handsome, rich, or intelligent you are, she'll eventually tire of it. So, you could choose to be a passive victim to this dynamic and blame your fights on her female "crazy" while waiting for *her* to change. Or you can acknowledge that the Feminine needs to feel emotionally connected to her man in order to feel settled and open. To participate in that you need to know and share your own feelings.

Furthermore, your emotions are signals to you about your own inner wounds, fears, and dysfunctions. Ignorance only means that these things drive your behavior in ways you won't understand. You will live life reactively rather than out of conscious choice.

So, **the reason to learn your emotions is NOT so you can be a "new age evolved" man or a "good" man, but rather so you can be a powerful man**. Not because society or your woman say you should, but because you would rather lead your woman into openness rather than wallow in a fight.

EXPRESSING YOUR EMOTION

Sharing your emotions is not about vomiting all of your feelings and fears onto your intimate partner. It is simply self-knowledge, judiciously revealed when it serves to create more closeness with others. See the case of John:

John was married to an intense woman who was prone to anger. He had been recently laid off from a lucrative job in the technology sector and was searching for employment. One day during this time frame, his wife was upset at him because he hadn't been helping around the house. During an extended argument, she said: "If you aren't adding any value around here by making money you could at least do the laundry." Whoa. She went for the jugular on that one. John reacted without thinking: "I'm trying as hard as I can. You never support me! Why do you have to be such a bitch?!"

Of course, we know where that type of response will lead — nowhere. But he had another option, one which involved knowing his emotions in the moment. He could have turned his attention inward for a minute and realized that he felt hurt by her comment. He was already feeling shame over not working — her comment made it worse. In a calm voice, with solid eye contact, he might just have said *"Ouch"*, and nothing more. Or, he could have added: *"That hurts. I already feel a little shame around my employment situation. I need your support, not your taunting."*

He need not attack or make demands. He doesn't have to withdraw or become passive-aggressive. Rather, he knows that he feels hurt by her comment and feels shame about his job situation. And he shares it. It is this type of response that usually stops the other person in their tracks and opens up their compassion. That is what being in touch with your emotions looks like.

Unfortunately, men usually aren't that skillful. You clam up and claim *"I don't feel anything"* or *"I'm fine."* The Masculine archetype in your head doesn't include emotional expression, so you tell yourself "*That's not what men do.*" To you, wallowing in emotion feels like just spinning in a circle when you should be just getting on with life. It feels like a self-indulgent waste of time, antithetical to the Masculine's goal orientation.

But this tendency just covers up the real reason: men suppress their emotions to avoid the sense of threat that arises in various parts of life. In John's case, his wife's cutting comment induced shame in him, which was rooted in a belief that he was inadequate (because he wasn't earning money) and that his wife would be less attracted to such a man. That threatened his relationship. It would be much easier to shut down and say "*I'm fine*" or blast anger at her than it would be to admit his shame and fear.

That was certainly the case in this example from a client:

> *Stephen had been going through a long rocky period with his wife. One day he sent an email to several of us in his inner circle that said: "Today my wife and I agreed to a divorce during a counseling session. In this moment I do not feel relief nor sadness or regret. I just feel calm and centered. I have a feeling of gratitude toward myself and her. And it's time to move on."*

We talked shortly after that, and I asked him about his state of calm. Honestly, I was skeptical that he wasn't feeling other emotions as well. The minute he started denying that he did, I knew he was suppressing something because he felt tight to me. By our third conversation that week, he ended up breaking down in our session, overcome as he opened to the pain and fear he felt about becoming single again. He didn't know what that looked like and whether he'd be alone for the rest of his life. He also expressed deep regret about the impact on his children. I immediately felt closer to him because he finally owned what I'd sensed in him. I encouraged him to say out loud that he felt scared of being alone. Simply acknowledging that fear (without even doing anything to change it) took away much of its power over him. He felt much more relaxed to me, and shared that he felt less scared now. And it opened him up to start the process of addressing his fear through inner work. Through that work, he was more ready to re-enter the dating world in his full power.

This breakthrough and release of some of his fear would never have happened in his "*I'm fine*" mode.

Ignorance or denial of your emotions will keep you trapped in them. And it will not open your woman. Quite frankly, I feel sorry for most women having to put up with us men. Either we say we feel nothing, or we get mad and blame them. Or we claim not to be mad at all and just covertly punish them with coldness or passive-aggressive behavior. Feminine people feel EVERYTHING and have to learn to live with men who have no idea what to do with their own emotions. They end up feeling catastrophically unmet. And we wonder why they seem to complain more and want sex less. They feel abandoned when we shut down. They feel our suppressed anger as aggression. And they feel the weakness of a man who can't simply say what he feels while staying grounded and present.

This act of openly sharing what you feel inside is commonly known as "being vulnerable". Because guys see these emotions as signs of weakness, to acknowledge them to yourself and others is scary. You spent your entire life building up your defenses so you didn't have to feel these emotions. So revealing them feels like you are pulling down those defenses, and thus you are literally "vulnerable".

But the incredibly ironic part of this is that **while you may see this sharing as weakness, women see your emotional vulnerability (when done skillfully) as STRENGTH**. In their eyes, only a strong man can reveal these types of feelings. It is the weak man that tries to posture and always appear rock solid and together. And remember, women feel everything, so you aren't going to fool them. You'll just be proving your unworthiness.

I speak from experience here. I've hesitated to share many feelings over the years with my woman, worried that she'd think less of me. Somehow, each time I do share them, she feels closer to me and opens to me. My male brain still finds it odd, but I've learned to override that instinct now.

In fact, when you are authentic and vulnerable, EVERYONE feels closer to you. There is something about a guy that either seems like he has no problems or negative emotions that makes it difficult for people to connect with him. When you show a few cracks in the armor by being real, suddenly people find themselves more drawn to you because you feel more human. **It is so ironic — you reveal things that you think will cause people to judge you negatively, yet somehow they seem to like you more**.

COVERING OTHER EMOTIONS

Sometimes anger can cover up deeper emotions and prevent you from being aware of them. I'll illustrate through an example from a client:

Jarrod's girlfriend consistently shows up late when meeting him. It was consistent enough that he began to get angry about it. On the nights she would be late, he would feel himself a little bit more withdrawn the rest of the night. After tolerating this behavior for many months, he'd finally hit his limit and, one night angrily lectured her about it. He told her she wasn't respecting his time or showing him the common courtesy to show up on time. He was a busy person, so he usually had to stop working on important projects in order to meet her for their dates, so it was upsetting to show up and have to wait for her. He demanded that it stop. And, from a factual standpoint, he was justified in what he was asking. But she came away from this conversation in a state of shutdown. She respected that he was at least able to own his anger. But her Feminine intuition told her that something was missing. She couldn't feel the real him in his expression. So she felt a little disconnected from him after this conversation.

As he shared this story with me, I also felt the facts didn't fully explain his reaction, either the withdrawal or the anger. His reaction felt more like someone who was feeling hurt or scared, rather than that of someone laying down a boundary. As we dug into it, he began to realize that his subconscious was interpreting her lateness as a sign that their time together wasn't a high priority for her. That she cared about other things more than spending time with him. He was excited to get together and would arrange his day around it. Her lateness made him think she wasn't as excited. Otherwise, she would be on time. In his mind's eye, he envisioned her carelessly taking her time at the store, running an extra errand, or chatting with a friend. He projected on her that she knew all of this was making her late, but she didn't care. Which therefore stoked his fears that the relationship wasn't as important to her as it was to him.

This was a big shift in his self-awareness. His anger was justified — her tardiness was, in fact, careless and rude. But it was incomplete because it left out the feelings underneath. Directing only anger at your woman (*"You're always late!" "You don't respect my time!"*) may change her behavior, but it rarely creates more connection. The cold shoulder is even less effective. **But sharing what's underneath is far more effective at creating lasting change and opening up your heart-centered Feminine partner.**

Now, contrast this with a different way that Jarrod <u>might</u> have handled things. From a grounded place and with strong eye contact, Jarrod could share his inner state: *"I get angry when you're late. I know it seems crazy but sometimes it makes me think I'm not important to you or you don't enjoy our time together enough."* And that's it. Alternate Jarrod knows his feelings, and simply states them while staying in connection with his woman. He doesn't attack, lecture, withdraw, or hide. He simply shares.

This "Alternate Jarrod" did a lot of things right. He didn't commit the common Masculine mistake of going into a withdrawal state. This is usually the only way we can cope when we're suppressing the underlying feelings. The problem is that your woman will feel it immediately. She may try to ignore it or tolerate it for a while. She may ask you *"Are you feeling OK tonight?"*, to which you'll say that you're "fine". But it won't fool her. Women read these suppressed emotions as if they're written on our forehead. And it is said that any emotion we choose not to feel will have to be felt by those around us. If you don't acknowledge and feel your anger or fear or shame, your woman will have to feel it for you. It is painful for them when you don't own your emotions. It is the path of a child, not a man. Rather than stand strong and share what's real, you hide yourself.

Alternate Jarrod also shared his anger, but he didn't make it THE thing. It was only a beacon for him to what was going on underneath. He made the stuff underneath THE thing, and shared it vulnerably. That's a lot more effective.

Let me repeat this one for emphasis: definitely express your anger, but don't make it the primary part of the expression.

Notice what Alternate Jarrod did *not* do: demand anything from his woman. In sharing his feelings, he only stated how he felt. This is **extremely significant** because it illustrates a major difference between navigating your feelings in a Masculine way vs. doing so weakly: **if you share your feelings but NEED the other person to change or do something to help you feel OK, then you are operating out of weakness**. It is OK to WANT things to be different. It is not OK to NEED others to change.

Demanding that others change comes partially from having a "victim mentality". The shame, blame, and anger you share have one underlying message: "*You did this to me.*" It conveys that she needs to change in order to make things right and not have you feel this way. You might be factually correct about things, as was original Jarrod, and thus feel very justified in your approach. But I must say that in all my years on this earth, I have yet to see this approach open a woman up and have her feel closer. **She's more likely to either fight back, or to comply but actually feel closed inside**. Underneath, it feels to her that you won't be OK unless she molds herself to protect your wounds and insecurities as if she were Mommy. She won't perceive you as a powerful man who rules his own emotional world, but rather as a boy who blames others.

This is going to kill Polarity and attraction instantly. And it sure as hell won't motivate her to be different.

It's not that you don't want to share your anger. By all means, share it and own it. But when that is all that you share (which means you're blaming), it is not complete.

To avoid this, you can use an approach similar to the one we discussed earlier relative to sharing your anger — instead of "needing and demanding", you "share and own". The technique I'll share here is more generalized to cover any emotional response. You use the sentence stem of "*When you _____, it makes me feel _____.*" When the other person does a certain thing, it creates feelings in you. For Alternate Jarrod it was "*When you're late, I feel anxious because I think it is because our time is not important to you.*"

There are two primary elements in this approach:

1. The first part is an observation of something they said or did. It is irrefutable because it is merely a statement of fact, with no analysis, judgment, or labels attached to it.
2. The second part is simply a description of a feeling within you. This is also irrefutable because it is simply a fact that you do feel that way. As long as you are being truthful, no one can argue that you shouldn't feel that way.

Note that there is NO demand. It is simply an expression of what's true. And in the process, you are owning your feelings rather than dumping them on your partner. You are "speaking inarguably" because you are only saying what's true for you (which should be inarguable) rather than trying to characterize their motivations or what they SHOULD be doing (both of which can definitely be debated).

Let me reiterate for emphasis: of course you WANT other people to do things differently at times. I am not suggesting that you deny that desire. Just don't need it. I am not playing a word game here. Energetically the two are very different. Needing someone else to be different comes off as desperate and weak. This point is a major principle of Masculine leadership: **The Masculine man knows and shares his emotions without NEEDING anyone else to do anything or change in order to make the pain of those emotions stop**. He shares and he stops, and he bears any pain himself. This is fundamental to our core tenet of responding vs. reacting.

But guess what? Most humans are naturally empathetic beings. And, freed from your **demand** to change (which usually smuggles in your blaming and shaming of them), these humans often **choose** to modify their behavior in order to not create the negative feelings you are expressing. Without you even having to ask or demand! It is counterintuitive, but true nonetheless.

Now, having said all of this, you can still add a request on to the end of your expression, as we did with expressing anger. But I encourage you to just try it without that at first. See what you can evoke in your partner.

SHARE JUDICIOUSLY

Now, it is important that you do not swing too far and start oversharing your emotional state with others. **Remember that the Masculine must sometimes suffer in silence**. You don't need to share EVERY time you have an emotional reaction. Rather, my advice to you is to open up as needed. There are a few markers that I use that tell me openness is called for:

1. *If I'm angry at someone else, blaming them, and feeling like a victim.* It usually means I'm focusing on them at the exclusion of examining my own wounds, reactions, and insecurities.

2. *If I'm shutting down or going passive-aggressive.* This accomplishes nothing except to isolate me from other people and my own feelings.

3. *If my woman directly asks me what I'm feeling.* She usually asks when she feels me holding something back or simply wants to feel closer to me in general. Being vulnerable when she asks goes a long way toward opening her up to me, which is a state in which I like having her.

Outside of situations like these, I encourage you to keep your own counsel on your emotions. You should always *know* your emotions, but avoid *oversharing* them.

When you do choose to share, be brief. I recommend you **take what you are feeling and boil it down into two sentences** in the "*When you …*" format discussed earlier:

> *"When you complain about the size of the laundry room, I think you're criticizing me for not making enough money and that hurts. I get worried you don't respect me."*

> *"When you're late, I sometimes think our time is not important to you. Then I start thinking I'm not important to you and it scares me."*

"When you make comments about me not having a job right now, I think you are judging me. I worry that you think less of me."

Then, once you've expressed your two sentences, stop talking. Do not try to explain the entire context for the emotion or every nuance. It is critical to just keep it simple.

And whatever you do, **don't feel that you need to justify your emotions**. Facts can be defended. Logic can be defended. Emotions cannot and should not be defended. They are what they are. It is important that you don't feel the need to defend what you feel. It just spirals into an intellectual dissection of emotion, something for which she is far better equipped than you. If your woman tries to challenge your right to feel that way, just settle into the truth of what you've said and ask her if she can just take it in.

Having said that, I will also offer a caveat. You are a man. She is a woman, and she probably has the superpower of feeling emotion more than you. While what you've shared may be part of the truth, it might not be everything and she may point this out to you. So, **remain open that she may be able to help you discover some still unexpressed parts of your emotional state**. She may feel things that you don't. Your psyche is good at hiding things from yourself as much as from others. Let her be your mirror and your Oracle.

CONCLUSION

It is my ardent desire to shift your perception of the relationship between a strong man and his emotions. The Masculine man is not stoic, shutting down to all emotions like a rock. Any woman will tire of this.

Men of past generations were often stoic men, and the women in their life likely suffered for it.

Undiscovered, unacknowledged, and unexpressed emotions create reactivity in the form of withdrawal, denial, aggression, and nice guy behavior. Coming to terms with your emotions is the first and most powerful thing you can do to build the muscle of responding vs. reacting.

And furthermore, your woman is more likely to follow you if you are emotionally aware. She will feel met. She will trust you and, as a result, is more likely to open her heart and body to you. This is a big part of living from your Masculine core, and will be a powerful tool for you in leading your woman into more trust, lust, and devotion.

CHAPTER 10

EMBODIMENT

So far, we've discussed how to reduce anxiety and reactivity by understanding the role that threat plays, as well as becoming more skillful with your emotions. In this chapter, I'll share with you a variety of somatic practices that use meditation, breath, and movement to bring you into your body. Each is intended to increase your nervous system's capacity for intensity and anxiety.

You've probably heard encouragement that you need to "get out of your head and into your body more" (which is what is meant by the phrase "embodiment"). This is a true statement, and it's an important one. Let's examine what it means.

This is a foundational topic relative to building your Masculine core, and one chapter is not nearly enough. You can go deeper into these practices in my book *The Art of Embodiment for Men* and the companion online video course. See the appendix for more information.

LOST IN YOUR HEAD

Modern life involves a constant flow of information into your brain. We all consume endless amounts of content through our phones — emails, texts, articles, audio, and video. It puts you into your thinking mind and traps you there. Over time, this consumption strengthens that thinking mind, just as exercise would strengthen a muscle. It grows so strong that your thoughts start to become your entire reality.

Your awareness of your "feeling body" fades over time. And because your instincts, emotions, and primal nature all exist at the body level, you progressively lose access to these elements when you're trapped in your thinking mind.

You can't hear your instincts. You can't feel and process your emotions. And you can't tap into your primal power.

All you can do is think and analyze. The torrent of thoughts become your entire reality. Absent a strong connection to your instincts, emotions, and primal nature, the signals of the mind loom largest. They take the form of stories you project onto the world.

An example of this would be when your woman is criticizing you. You get triggered, think to yourself "*Why is she being such a bitch?*", and then may react from that place. But her "being a bitch" is just a story that your mind generates to explain away your confusion about why she's suddenly being so critical, and to protect yourself from the anxiety you feel as a result of her criticism. When you're lost in that story, you can't feel your love for her. You're not fully present. You can't objectively recognize the anxiety within you. You lose touch with your Masculine core. You can't rely on your primal nature as a source of strength.

And **you sure as hell can't feel her pain**, which is what she's actually craving from you. All you can do is remain lost in the story your mind has created.

But when you become more embodied, it breaks the tyranny of the thinking mind. Instead of your attention only being on thought signals, it can now rest on the physical, emotional, instinctual, and primal signals from the body. Using them as a reference point, you can now see through the illusion of the mind and its stories.

This happens because your attention focuses mainly on one source at a time. If the thinking mind is dominant, your stories get all of your attention. But by waking up your body, your physicality now comes into your field of attention, **literally crowding out the thoughts and giving you something else on which to focus.**

This naturally brings you more into the present moment for one simple reason: **thoughts are largely about past and future, but the body always exists in the now.** When you listen to the physical, emotional, instinctual, and primal signals based in the body more than the rampant thoughts in your mind, you live more in the actual reality that is happening in THIS moment. Not some reality manufactured out of stories of the past and worries about the future.

And when you're more embodied, you will also have more capacity for bodily sensation. In other words, you can handle more anxiety, which exists as an intense, unpleasant energy in the body. Just like you can build up muscles, you can develop this capacity through a consistent embodiment practice. **This is the most effective way to train your nervous system to handle more intensity.**

EMBODIMENT SAVES RELATIONSHIPS

The effects of an embodiment practice will be *powerful* in your relationship. Imagine your woman angry with you and complaining intensely. It feels unfair and also touches on a nerve around which you feel some subconscious shame. If you are thinking-dominant, you'll likely get triggered and lost in a story of the unfairness of her attack, as well as the subconscious mental exercise of suppressing or avoiding the feeling of shame. In that state, you won't be present.

But the more embodied you are, the better equipped you are to handle this intensity. You'll breathe deep and feel your body, which will naturally dampen the emotional triggers and cognitive stories. You'll be more present and realize that you're in no danger. From this place, you'll stay grounded and more available to hold space for her pain.

Embodiment provides a calm sanctuary from the chaos of your mind and the anxiety it produces. When your wounds and insecurities scream at you that you're not good enough, that you need a certain person's approval and validation, or that someone is going to leave you if you don't meet a specific need of theirs in this moment — this is when embodiment can make all the difference. **Your connection with your physical body will be like a trail of breadcrumbs leading you out of the illusion of your mind**. As you rest in the body, your attention will move from fixating on the mind and the anxiety to focusing on bodily sensations. The volume on the anxiety and the stories will be turned down.

Thoughts trigger emotions, and emotions trigger thoughts. It becomes a vicious cycle. Embodiment breaks that cycle, allowing you to just exist in the now.

Embodied men are naturally more grounded. Embodied men don't believe the stories — in their mind or in others' minds — quite as much. Embodied men are more resilient to anxiety and intensity. Embodied men just feel more solid to everyone around them.

The women can feel it the most. They just know the difference between a man who regularly engages in embodiment practices and one who doesn't. The man who doesn't, who is stuck in his mind, never feels fully present. Nor does he feel primal. For most women, it is much harder to be attracted to such a man.

You'll find that your woman's nervous system settles when you are in an embodied state.

THE IMPORTANCE OF REGULAR PRACTICE

The practices I share below will help you get into that state. They wake up the somatic sensations in your body. And some of them are specifically designed to help you increase your capacity to tolerate intensity. In the end, all of them should reduce the impact of anxiety on you.

Note that these activities are called "practices" for a reason. You must consistently perform them over time for them to have an effect. Single sessions have little lasting impact, just as one workout at the gym will not make you noticeably stronger. I encourage you to not simply try these a few times and lose interest because they're "not working". A couple of days of practice will yield nothing. A week of practice will give you tactical, short-lived benefit. Only months of consistent practice will create a lasting effect.

Remember that embodiment and knowledge are two different things. With knowledge, you read or hear about something, the light bulb goes on, and you have new capabilities based on your new understanding. It can happen quickly. But **knowledge alone is NOT enough to develop your Masculine core**. You can't just read a book and have it happen. **You MUST have an embodiment practice too**. If you are not willing to commit time to an ongoing and consistent embodiment practice, you won't get there. You should just put this book down now and abandon the effort. This cannot be solely a mental pursuit.

I struggled with being consistent with these practices when I was first introduced to them. My mentors were telling me they were important, but I just couldn't find my discipline around them. After some introspection, I finally realized that I was staying in my comfort zone, which was the mental aspects of Masculine development. But I had resistance to doing the somatic practices. Thankfully, this all changed when I started to see results, even from the little bit of practice I was doing. I liked this growing feeling of resting in bodily sensations, and how they dampened the impact of my mental narratives and resultant anxiety. I encourage you to follow the same path: make a commitment to get started, and eventually the results will come. Once they do, you'll be hooked.

The practices we'll discuss fall into four categories: meditation, breath, intensity expanders, and movement. Some of the practices come from long-standing traditions, and you can easily research them via other resources. Others, such as *Provocation Meditation* and *Intentioned Assertive Movement* are my proprietary practices, and they are covered in detail in *"The Art of Embodiment"*. My goal here is simply to expose you to a range of exercises and inspire you to take on a daily embodiment practice of your own.

MEDITATION PRACTICES

The first practice I will share is **basic meditation**. This is a topic well-covered by innumerable authors over many centuries. So I will focus on discussing how it maps into the context of this book.

Ultimately, meditation is a practice of separating from your thoughts so that you can observe them rather than being caught up in them. You stop experiencing them as an all-encompassing 'reality', but rather simply as arising phenomena that you can choose to believe or not believe.

As I said before, thoughts create emotions. So your thought 'reality', which may not match objective reality, creates a whole set of emotions within you. Then your mind makes up stories to make sense of the chaos of these emotions. You become a reactive mess of thoughts and emotions, each instigating the other.

Practicing meditation improves your ability to notice and separate from subconscious thought loops and stories. For instance, consider again the situation of your woman being mad at you. It's more than likely you have experienced some type of thought loop happening about her being unreasonable, that she always acts illogically, that your motives were pure and therefore her anger is unjustified. You'll have an emotional reaction to this, likely including your own anger. And then these emotions may get amplified by old memories of a parent who was angry with you (*"Uh oh, I'm in trouble ... "*), or stories about yourself based in some self-loathing (*"I always mess up ... "*). Meditation is going to help you notice the thoughts and stories arise and not get caught up in them as irrefutable truth to which you react.

Without a doubt, a daily meditation practice should be a core part of your daily practice. But, as it is taught in the mainstream, I feel there are two primary limitations.

First, I don't think there is enough emphasis on the use of physical sensations to help clear the mind of thoughts. As I said before, using the mind to govern the mind is quite difficult. But putting attention on physical sensation seems to clear the mind much more effortlessly.

Second, I think mainstream meditation does not emphasize the role of emotions enough. You might be able to use the mind to let go of boredom-related thought. But it is MUCH harder to use that technique to clear emotion-based ruminating thought.

I address both of these issues in *"The Art of Embodiment"* book and online course, where I help you understand the role of using both sensation and emotions in your meditation practice.

· · ·

In the *"Art of Embodiment"*, I take this even further through a unique practice called *Provocation Meditation.* Here, you are allowed to use the mind, via memories and visualizations, to stir up an emotional response within you. Then you let go of the story and simply feel the emotions that have been activated. You practice just sitting with them, and in the process you increase your capacity for intensity.

I created this practice out of my own experience of basic meditation being a little too clean. You certainly need to be able to notice and let go of your thoughts. But that is not enough, because when anxiety arises in real life, it is very difficult to let go of thoughts with the antagonist standing in front of you. So you need to practice developing your capacity to stay grounded while IN this triggered state.

Remember — it's easy for the wise man on top of the mountain to be grounded. But that "wise man" is usually fighting with his wife within five minutes of returning to real life. **It does you little good to learn how to become settled in a vacuum. You MUST learn to do it in the fire of interrelating.** You have to learn to ground yourself when, for instance, your woman (or anyone important to you) is in front of you, mad at you and breathing fire. It entails learning to speak or feel in the face of overwhelming anxiety and the urge to withdraw, shut down, or blame.

Again, see *"The Art of Embodiment"* for more information about this practice.

BREATH PRACTICES

The next set of practices involve the breath. The first is just a simple awareness practice around intentional breathing. All that is required is for you to slowly breath in and out, fully filling and emptying the lungs, and have all of your attention on the breath itself. Feel the fluid qualities of air as it slides across the inner part of your nostrils. Feel the rising of your chest and filling of your lungs as you inhale. Feel all of the physical sensations.

I recommend you do this with what is called an Ujjayi breath. This involves breathing through the nose (mouth closed) but slightly constricting the back of the throat so that you create an audible sound, similar to what you do when you whisper. Ujjayi has a long list of known benefits on the heart, brain, digestion, nervous system, and immune system that you can research. But personally, I like that it slows the flow of breath and makes breathing more conscious for me.

Breathing deeply also serves as a focal point for your attention, hopefully distracting you from the thoughts and stories that run through your mind. This is why breathing takes center stage in meditation — it helps you break the monopoly of your thoughts by giving you a physical sensation on which to focus.

One of the things I like about this simple practice is that it also reminds me of how clenched my body is. As my chest cavity expands, it reveals all of the places I hold tight. So I recommend that, along with the breathing, you include a full body scan to notice these places. This clenching is one of the body-mind's defenses against anxiety. But, ironically, it also has the effect of storing and perpetuating it. So a systematic unclenching of your body can go a long way in reducing anxiety.

Deep, conscious Ujjayi breathing is your secret weapon for settling your body chemistry. You can do it anytime — alone, in line at the grocery store, or in front of your upset partner. Use it liberally.

• • •

The next breath exercise is one I simply describe as a "lung expander". I'm not aware of its origins, but it is used in many domains. The practice is very simple. Take in a full breath and hold it. Then take two more sips of breath into the lungs to bring them to their absolute maximum capacity. Hold for five seconds and then release.

I also like to add a squeeze of the perineum during the five-second hold. It gives you something to do during the hold, and also brings sensation to and wakes up the genital region. Never a bad thing.

You will definitely feel the stretch in your lungs and chest cavity, and that is the point. You're trying to stretch your capacity for breath, just as you stretch your muscles before engaging in sports activities.

You are also teaching your body to relax. As you expand in this exaggerated way, it will reveal and relax the places in your torso that you subtly clench. Relax into them.

Perform this ten times in the morning, and again at night. In just a few days you'll start to feel the cumulative effects and your breath should start to become more effortless.

· · ·

The third exercise comes from Kundalini tradition and is called Breath of Fire. I've seen many promises associated with it: calming, detoxing, pain relieving, mentally invigorating, etc. The one claim I can make with confidence is that it absolutely wakes up my body if done consistently and vigorously. It focuses on the abdomen, solar plexus, and chest, which is where most of us hold a lot of tension. I've heard this called the "center channel" or "center column", something which we want to wake up. My experience is that Breath of Fire helps loosen tightness in these areas, thus allowing the energy to move.

To begin, take a big breath in, then consciously and slowly exhale through your nose. Get all of the air out. Take another full breath in, and then slowly but powerfully exhale out. Do it long enough to push ALL of the air out. You should feel your diaphragm (at the lowest part of your belly) pushing during this exhale. That is what you will use to power this Breath of Fire.

Now, instead of using the diaphragm to push out a long *slow* breath, you are now going to push out the breath very quickly. You'll use the diaphragm like a pump. Try it now. Squeeze it to pump a quick outbreath through the nose. Do a continuous series of these, at a pace somewhere between five breaths every three seconds to two every second.

Focus solely on the outbreath. Let the inbreath happen of its own accord. It will become automatic, enough to keep up with the pace you set for the outbreaths.

This is intended to be a very physical exercise. Strongly engage the diaphragm, it will make your entire torso move with each powerful outbreath. No small, tepid breaths. Do it with intensity.

This practice will bring blood flow and sensation to a part of the body that is chronically clenched and numb for most people. I encourage you to persist through the intensity. It gets better over time if you are consistent.

Start with thirty seconds, and perform this practice daily. Move up to several minutes as you acclimate to the intensity. I recommend always using a timer. Otherwise, you'll find yourself quitting early. Just let the timer take charge and tell you when to finish.

You can find plenty of resources on the Breath of Fire via a simple internet search.

• • •

The fourth breath exercise I will share with you is called Wim Hof breathing, created by a man literally named Wim Hof. Like with the Breath of Fire, you can find all the resources you need on the internet, and I encourage you to do so. Here I will simply provide a short introduction.

Wim Hof breathing starts with a rapid inbreath as if you are sucking through a straw, and fills the lungs to 100 percent. The outbreath then flows organically of its own accord, and empties to 20 percent capacity. It is the opposite of Breath of Fire, which placed the intention and effort on the *outbreath* and had an organic *inflow*.

This method involves performing thirty of these breaths, optimally at around one per second. Do them with a lot of physicality. Make these breaths **assertive**. This maximizes the sensation and "wakes up" the torso area.

Right after the thirtieth inhale, exhale fully and sit with empty lungs for up to forty-five seconds. This is hard to do, so you may have to work up to this duration. Then, at forty-five seconds or when you can't hold it any longer, draw a **full** inbreath and again hold for up to forty-five seconds.

Like Breath of Fire, Wim Hof breathing serves to bring sensation and activation to the belly, solar plexus, and chest areas. And the holding of the breath can increase your lung capacity. It is for these reasons, at a minimum, that I recommend this practice.

Beyond this, Wim Hof and his adherents make a number of significant claims about other benefits. I leave it to the reader to research these.

INTENSITY EXPANDERS

The next group of practices is intended to create a significant amount of discomfort in your body. You do them specifically to increase your nervous system's capacity to handle physical intensity. Which, in turn, maps over into your capacity to handle the emotional intensity of relational stress and anxiety. Build this capacity and you *will* increase your ability to be grounded in the face of relationship challenges.

The first practice I'll share is called the Ego Eradicator. The core practice comes from Kundalini tradition.

You can do this exercise sitting or standing in a slight Horse Stance. Raise your arms up at a sixty-degree angle (relative to the ground) out to the sides. Your body will be in the shape of the letter "Y". The arms are straight, the fingers are curled in to touch the palms, and the thumbs are straight out like a hitchhiker's.

Now begin Breath of Fire, and hold the arms above you throughout the breathing phase.

This gets very difficult rather quickly. Thirty seconds is usually no problem, but when you get up to three minutes and beyond, most people have a very hard time keeping their arms at that angle above the head. You will start to shake. You will start feeling intense pain. Your mind will scream at you to lower your arms.

That voice in your head that tells you to lower the arms is the same voice that tells you to do something to make your relationship anxiety stop. The intense sensation in your arms is equivalent to the bodily sensation of anxiety that you find intolerable. In this exercise, you're increasing your capacity for intensity in one domain so that it is available for you in the other. It maps over.

As you feel the intensity from holding up your arms, picture in your mind your woman in front of you with eyes blazing in anger at something you've done. Picture "that look" that she gives you, as well as the disgusted tone of voice that you probably know well. Let that merge with the actual pain and intensity you are feeling in the moment from the exercise.

Then, in the midst of all of that, find the place in yourself that can withstand the physical pain and intensity, that won't listen to the inner voice that demands you quit or make it stop. You will be strengthening the same capability that allows you to stay grounded, present, and connected in the midst of the pain and intensity created in you by your woman's anger. Or any intensity in life.

I recommend that you hold your arms up for three minutes at first, and work your way up to ten minutes and beyond. It is critical for you to get to a point where your body is rebelling (within constraints of common sense and safety, of course) and you have the overwhelming impulse to drop your arms. This is similar to doing weight lifting sets until exhaustion — you have to suffer a little in order to grow your capacity. And, of course, consult a health professional before engaging in any intense physical activity.

Again, I encourage you to use a timer rather than just going until you can no longer stand it. The timer will keep you disciplined.

If you believe in the core theme of this book — that anxiety is at the root of nearly all non-Masculine behavior — then this is a critical life-long practice for you.

• • •

The next practice is a visualization that you can add to the Wim Hof breathing that I mentioned before. After thirty seconds of holding your breath, the intensity will eventually start to induce panic. In this state, your practice is to pretend you are drowning. Imagine yourself unable to escape the water, and see if you can mentally surrender into that scenario. Can you settle into the panic and die with dignity in this visualization? If you can achieve that state of relaxation, then you'll be able to resist the voice that screams at you to take a breath. And if you can do that, then you'll be growing your capacity to resist that voice that tells you to defend yourself from your woman's attacks, to withdraw or give her the cold shoulder, to close your heart, or to give in and forgo your own needs in order to make the intensity stop.

So in the context of this exercise, surrender into your envisioned demise and extend the amount of time that you can hold your breath.

• • •

The next practice is to participate in something called a sweat lodge, a tradition with roots in Native American peoples. It is something you should only do with a trained facilitator, or else it can be dangerous. It is usually performed in a low canvas dome. Participants sit in a circle around a central pit in which very hot rocks are placed. A trained facilitator leads you through several rounds of chanting and storytelling. The entire ceremony was originally designed for prayer and healing.

Like the Ego Eradicator and holding your breath, there is an endurance component that is relevant to your quest to expand your nervous system capacity. This comes from the fact that the dome will be incredibly hot, cramped (you will typically have other participants pressed up against you on both sides), and dark. Heat and claustrophobia will create an intensity that is challenging for most people to handle.

Your mind may scream that you must get out of that dome. That the heat is too much. That you'll become trapped by the close quarters and disoriented by the darkness. All three will conspire to challenge you as you've never been challenged before.

And it is this state in which you'll grow your nervous system capacity. Like the other practices, you'll learn to ignore the voice that screams that you're not safe. To breath deeply, to self-soothe. And in this case, you won't have the option to simply drop your arms or release your breath to make the intensity stop. Although you could certainly just get up and exit the sweat lodge, both the people pressed tightly on both sides of you and unspoken peer pressure will be a barrier to you quitting the practice. So you'll have to endure it, and in the process, you'll grow your capacity for intensity.

This has certainly been the case for me — every time I do one I experience some level of panic from the heat, darkness, and tight quarters. But each one has pushed my envelope a little further. It is a practice I highly recommend. But be certain to check with your doctor that your health can support this activity, and always do your sweat with an experienced and properly trained facilitator.

MOVEMENT PRACTICES

The next group of practices involves movement of the body. These are intended to activate the body and, in doing so, liberate you from your mind.

The first category I will share is not a practice per se, but an encouragement to make embodied practices such as team sports, yoga, or dance a consistent part of your life. Anything that primarily uses the body, and only uses the mind's instincts rather than its cognitive capabilities. Such movement activities are the antithesis of being lost in information in your head. Make them part of your regular lifestyle.

Having said this, martial arts top the list of activities in terms of the ability to bring you back into your body. The context of combat serves to raise your adrenaline level. Seeking to hit another human brings out your aggression. Being hit by another certainly creates a lot of sensation in the body. And finally, the confidence and sense of safety derived from practicing your combat skills serve to make you more comfortable in your own skin.

All of this was my experience when I started studying Krav Maga, a particularly violent Israeli martial art. I highly recommend this for you. You'll feel your body more and likely experience an organic boost in your physical confidence.

The reality is that modern life puts us in front of our phones and computers for far too many hours in a day. We become information processing creatures rather than physical creatures. We exist in our mind rather than use our bodies. You MUST counter this with a regular practice of strenuous physical activity.

• • •

Now, I'd like to introduce you to a practice of my own creation: *Intentioned Assertive Movement*. It is rather straightforward, but surprisingly powerful in a number of ways. It is partially inspired by the slow, intentional breath and movements of Tai Chi and Qi Gong. It is a standing practice that involves a basic push-pull movement of the arms, synched up with your breathing.

First and foremost, this exercise builds your capacity to move with Intention. The Masculine doesn't take actions that aren't consciously chosen, so IAM is designed to strengthen this capability in you. It does this by requiring that you explicitly choose in your mind to make a movement before you actually perform that movement. And you keep choosing to stay in motion until you consciously choose to stop that motion. This is an important and effective practice in cultivating the Masculine quality of deliberateness.

On top of this are added layers of the practice that use visualization to help you build your capacity for asserting yourself over others, something with which every Pleaser Nice Guy could use some help.

This is an extremely powerful and effective practice that is fully presented in *"The Art of Embodiment"*. It has become a core piece of my own daily practice.

CONCLUSION

I will repeat something I said earlier: developing your Masculine power is not solely a cognitive path, but rather one that requires regular (i.e. daily) embodiment practices. Doing this takes a big commitment of your time and attention. It requires discipline, but I assure you that the payoff is worth it.

And let me be clear — these embodiment practices are not some "woo-woo" activity. Their effects are very real, very explainable, very attainable, and very impactful. And indispensable for your path of developing your ability to respond rather than react.

ELEMENT 2

PROVIDE **STRUCTURE**

In this section, we will explore the second element of a Masculine core: providing structure in your relationship and the world around you.

When you do this, you give your woman something around which to orient, which helps her relax into your lead.

In order to provide structure successfully, you must first know what it is that YOU want. In Chapter 11, we explore how to tap deeply into your own desires. This sets the stage for a deep exploration of how to provide direction and structure in Chapter 12. We then finish with a challenging area for many men: taking charge in the bedroom. You will learn to master the art of leading your woman to her own pleasure.

DESIRE

Women find it sexy when a man knows what he wants. The clarity feels very Masculine to them, and is a foundational piece of the *Blueprint* I am presenting. **You can't lead your relationship unless you have your own views, opinions, preferences, needs, and boundaries**.

The clarity of being tapped into your desire is also a strong antidote to anxiety. It **trains your nervous system to focus on inner signals rather than trying to frantically please everyone else** by chasing **their** desires.

NO OPINION MEANS NO CONFLICT?

It's common for men to fall into the rut of going along with whatever their woman wants in the mistaken belief that this is the easiest path to her happiness and, therefore, relationship bliss. The subconscious comes to believe that no opinion means no conflict.

Sadly, it usually has the opposite effect. For years you give your woman what she says she wants. You subjugate your opinion to hers. You go to the places she wants to go, do the things she wants to do, wear the clothes she suggests you wear. You change your opinions to match hers.

"*Whatever you want, honey.*" Maybe, deep down, you just want your good-little-boy head patted for being so responsive to her (of course, you don't think of it this way, but sometimes that's what it is). Maybe you've just become lazy and now habitually take what seems like the path of least resistance. Or maybe you just see yourself as an easy-going guy.

Whatever the reason, over time she will become more and more frustrated that you seem to lack the fundamental Masculine qualities of direction and clarity.

If you want to lead, you'd better be in touch with your own needs and desires. This includes well-developed opinions on what you want and like, such as where you want to eat dinner, what you want her to wear, how you think the kids should be disciplined, how to handle home maintenance, how to resolve dilemmas that arise, or even specifically how you want her to crawl across the bed to you before you make love. It would also include your boundaries, such as how much time you can commit to helping her with a project before you need to get back to finishing up your own work, how she speaks to you when she's angry, or how often you need to take time away from family to exercise. As a man, you need to know what you want, know what you need, and know your boundaries.

Notice that I said you are not demanding any of these things. You are simply stating your desires and boundaries. From there she can make any choice she wants. This is **desire**, not **control**.

Why does your woman find it so sexy when you're strongly in touch with these things? Because they give her a fulcrum around which to orient. When you're opinionless, you're essentially formless. She doesn't know where you stand and how her needs and desires impact you. The Feminine feels uncomfortable without this kind of structure. So she's forced into her Masculine so she can create the structure she needs. As a result, she trusts you and your lead less.

LACK OF DESIRE IN ACTION

Let's look at some examples of not being in touch with your own desires:

- You and your woman are getting ready for a holiday party. She asks for your opinion about which of two dresses you'd like her to wear that night. You look up, and without even a pause you say "*I think they both look great. Whichever one you like.*"
- You and your woman decide to go out to dinner. She asks "*Where do you want to go?*" and you respond with "*I don't know. Where do you want to go?*" Then it ping pongs back and forth between the two of you.
- Your woman asks you to pick her up after work because she doesn't want to pay the cost for an Uber across town. While it might save $25, it will also take thirty minutes of your time and you're feeling crunched at work. But you don't want to disappoint her so you reluctantly agree but are annoyed the entire time.
- You and your wife are discussing how to handle your fifteen-year-old child's plummeting grades. Your wife is emotional about the whole thing and is frantically throwing out ideas about getting him a tutor, changing schools, taking away his phone, and grounding him on weekends. You aren't adding any ideas to the discussion, but say "*Those are all good ideas, Honey. If that's what you want to do.*" She suddenly lashes out at you in anger — "*Why don't you have any ideas!?*" — and you're shocked because you thought you were being supportive and collaborative.

- You are single, and at a party you see a woman whose radiance catches your attention. You would very much like to meet her but don't know if she'd be interested in you at all. You keep looking for signals that would give you "permission" to engage — eye contact, a smile, anything. You end up never approaching. Your desire to meet her cannot seem to overcome your need for some sign of permission.

Each of these is an example of not being in touch with your own desire. In each case, you're deferring to another. Sometimes even when your woman is clearly asking for your opinion. "*Whatever you want...*" somehow becomes the default response for so many men. But this is what you say to your drinking buddies, not the woman you want to lead.

When you decline to offer opinions or desires, she's forced into her own Masculine in order to make a decision either for herself or for the couple. She has to decide which dress to wear. She needs to decide tonight's restaurant. She has to decide how to handle your child's study habits. Even the woman at the party is forced into this position — if any conversation is going to happen, she's going to have to be the one to make the first move.

Your lack of expressed desire is depolarizing. The Feminine wants to surrender into your leadership, clarity, and decisiveness, not drift in your indecisiveness.

Lacking these Masculine gifts from you, she's abandoned to make her own decisions in situations where she's clearly asked for your opinions or guidance. If you're not in a state of certainty, then she's pushed into a state of uncertainty. It's agonizing for a Feminine woman to be in that state with a man. As David Deida teaches, over time she'll start relying on her own Masculine direction since she's learned not to expect yours.

So, remember this: **asking your woman what she wants and giving it to her is the opposite of Masculine leadership.** It will neither create Polarity nor make her happy over the long haul.

So when your woman asks you for your opinion about a dress, have one. Lazily deferring to what she might prefer is, for lack of a better term, lame. Sure, you may think that both dresses look equally great and you'd be happy with either. But she perceives your lack of preference very differently. To her, it is a signal that you're *not interested* in how she looks. That is not going to make her feel loved and desired by you. Nor will she feel appreciated in her efforts to look pretty for you.

In the second example, your woman is clearly signaling to you that she is in a state of indecision around a dinner location, yet you blow off the signal and lob the decision back to her. She's teeing up an opportunity for you to lead her and create more Polarity, yet you whiff on it. Keep that up and you can safely assume that in a few years she'll be just telling you what to do, having given up on the possibility of you leading her.

In the third example, your woman is asking for something that you actually don't want to do, and you're not willing to set a boundary. So you subjugate your own needs to hers. You might be gaining short term harmony but giving up the long-term respect that a woman has for a man who can say "*No*".

In the fourth example, your woman is looking to you for both leadership and simple collaboration. She's in an emotional state because of her deep Feminine care for her child. And while she's able to talk intelligently on the topic, she could use some grounding and structure from you. Your woman is also looking for your ideas and engagement on the matter. She doesn't want to feel like she has to come up with all of the answers because it will make her feel lonely and unpartnered in the raising of your child. The ideas, structure, and directionality you bring to the table are her evidence that she's not in this alone.

The final example is a little different because it about someone not in relationship, and this book is for men in relationship. But the situation is illustrative of my point. This is an example of where the desire to meet the woman is dwarfed by the fear that she's not open to it. As this man fixates on what SHE wants, he completely loses touch with what HE wants. Now, I'm not talking about crossing lines of consent in approaching this woman. This is much more innocent — he simply wants to meet her. But all he can think about is whether or not she would be interested in him. He's completely lost touch with his own desire to meet her.

To the logical mind, it can be hard to understand why men abdicate their desire. You probably don't even realize how much you do this. I invite you to start noticing the ways in which you haven't fully formed your own likes, preferences, and boundaries.

Threat and anxiety play a part. Life experience may have shown you that it is not safe to have needs and opinions. Maybe as a child, your parents got fed up with you reading under your covers after bedtime yet again, and punished you aggressively. You were just an innocent kid excited about a book, but they shut you down hard.

Or maybe you expressed some resistance about the creepy babysitter with whom you didn't feel comfortable. But your parents ignored your concern. They told you to quit worrying.

Childhood episodes like these, which are quite common, lead to your nervous system absorbing fear or shame around having needs.

And now here you are as an adult, face to face with your woman in one of the situations given in the earlier examples. You see yourself as a man who typically knows what he wants. But somehow there seems to be an invisible headwind arising, holding you back from claiming what it is that you truly want. This is the anxiety. It gently nudges you to stay quiet about your needs, opinions, and boundaries.

You do this because you fear making her upset. Your subconscious mind believes that if you are frank about what you want, it will create conflict that will cause your partner to be upset with you. Deep down, you're afraid your truth will cause you to lose her love and approval.

You also may fear rejection. The "wanting" of the desire gets inextricably intermixed with the "getting" of the desire. **You don't want to experience the disappointment of not "getting" what you want, so you subconsciously just suppress the "wanting".** You're so attached to the outcome that you throw the baby out with the bathwater.

So even in your best moments, you're choosing and editing your words carefully. You make tentative and half-hearted suggestions, rather than clear statements, in order to assess her opinion without having to commit.

Over time, you gradually lose touch with your needs entirely and they become invisible to you. It just becomes habit. And as this capability atrophies, you begin to second guess all of your instincts and become chronically indecisive about what you actually want in this life.

DESIRE IS POWERFUL

Contrast what I've described with the man who naturally orients to what he wants, likes, and dislikes. His attention is not on anxiously trying to decipher what everyone else wants. He's spent years cultivating his connection to his own needs. Hopefully he's not a narcissist, but rather someone who balances a strong adherence to his own desires with the needs and well-being of others.

He knows he can't serve others until he attends to his own basic needs.

This man uses his desire as an opportunity to create more Polarity in his relationship. When his woman asks him which dress he likes, his answer is not lukewarm. After pausing for effect, he might say: "*Hmm. The blue one looks good. But you look absolutely hot in the red one. I'm going to have to bring my stick to beat back the guys hitting on you.*" This man is giving a clear preference. The Feminine thrives on this. It provides structure for her.

But he goes further when he says she looks "hot", and uses humor to playfully emphasize the point. In the process of sharing his preference, he conveys appreciation of her beauty and uses humor, two things the Feminine also loves. What started as a minor question was leveraged into a powerful opportunity to create Polarity.

This is a man who also knows that his woman asks his opinion about where to eat because she's feeling a little indecisive herself. Her Feminine is craving his Masculine clarity in that moment.

He's also the one who sets a boundary and tells his woman *"No, I can't pick you up because I'm really crunched at work this week. We'll need to meet up later tonight."* She may not like the answer, but her Feminine side will deeply appreciate the clarity and honesty around what he needs.

He is the man who doesn't lazily leave the parenting ideas to his wife, but rather engages his brain and formulates his own ideas and perspectives and brings them to the table.

And he is the man whose desire to meet the beautiful woman wins out over his fear that she might not be interested in talking to him. He gives it a shot and approaches.

The Masculine knows what it wants because it doesn't lose touch with desire. If you want to bring leadership to your relationship, you need to know what YOU want. And have the strength of conviction to pursue it. This is a muscle you must strengthen over time.

The first step in this process is to **separate out the "wanting" of the desire from the "getting"**. Make these two distinct experiences. And then learn to become a connoisseur of the "wanting". Deepen your capacity to feel the strength of your desire. Revel in the pleasure you get from simply wanting something. Give yourself full permission to do so.

By way of example, I invite you to look across the room at a beautiful woman. It doesn't matter whether you're already partnered — this is just an exercise. Envision yourself engaging her (in an appropriate and consensual way), whether in conversation, tango dancing, or sexual play. Savor the visceral pleasure of the experience. And at no time give any thought as to whether that would happen, how that would happen, or whether she would accept or reject you. Just enjoy the wanting, feel it pulsing inside of you.

Smile to yourself as you experience the pleasure of it in your mind. The pleasure of wanting something can stand on its own, separate from the experience of it actually happening. It becomes its own satisfying experience, enough that you become less attached to the outcome and the object of your desire. This will free you up to stay in touch with the wanting without suppressing it to protect yourself from the pain of not getting it. Ironically, **letting go of the "getting" actually increases the chance of it happening because you won't be driven by neediness**.

Letting go of the "getting" part frees you up to acknowledge what you really want, unimpeded by probabilities of success. Even when you're <u>sure</u> the other person won't share your desire, KNOW what it is that YOU want, and be OK with it (again, assuming appropriateness here). You might not get it, but you won't let it diminish your wanting it.

Until, of course, reality dictates that you let go of the desire for your own well-being. Then you surrender into that reality.

This is cultivating your ability to be unattached to outcome. This is a process of training your nervous system to relax into all possibilities. The only thing you can do is bring the truth of your desire into the world. To lay it out for you and others to see. Everyone else will make their own independent choice in response. You need not grasp so tightly to what might happen.

You will start to see that **this capability looks a lot like confidence**, even though confidence and knowing what you want are two different things. A friend of mine shared a story which illustrates this well:

"I had just met my future wife, and back then she didn't seem particularly interested in me. I found her so alluring, but on our first two dates she was a bit aloof. I have to admit that I thought she was a bit out of my league. On our fourth date, we were laughing and she said 'You're so confident. I keep not calling you back and you keep asking me out.' He said 'Confident? I'm not confident at all. Every time I see you I think it's going to be the last time. The only thing I know is that I keep wanting to see you again.' She playfully hit me on the arm, and her voice dropped to a whisper 'That is confidence.' Two years later we were married."

Sometimes, the word 'confidence' is interpreted as a belief in a specific outcome. What I'm describing is different. It is about **being 100 percent sure of what you want, even when you have no idea what will actually happen**. The two look very much the same to the outside world, as the story above illustrates.

So if you want to project an air of confidence, just **want what you want** and keep pursuing it.

For instance, when the man in the example approaches the woman at the party, he has no way of knowing if she's open to him or if it will lead anywhere. But he can be rock solid in being **sure** that he wants to get to know her a bit more. That sureness is rooted in him being tapped into his desire.

Likewise, in speaking your truth to your woman, you have no idea how she will receive it, so you just stay rooted that whatever you're saying is in fact 100 percent true for you.

You're operating as if there's nothing to lose because you're not fixated on her acceptance or the outcome of the situation. You are totally open to both her Yes and her No. You will accept and honor either — and still want what you want. She may, in fact, be a complete and utter No to you, and it doesn't change a thing.

This is different than actual confidence. But to everyone else, it sure feels like confidence.

When you share your desires, do so without attachment to the outcome. Even when you expect resistance, you can do this. It may sound like: *"I'm not sure if you'd be a Yes or a No to this, but here's what I'm wanting. Would that work for you?"* By being this transparent, you immediately reduce the stakes of how the other person responds.

SELFISHNESS AND TRUTH

Your quest to tap into your desire requires you to develop an unexpected quality: selfishness. The word has a negative connotation. But what if selfishness were a virtue? What if we viewed it simply as a commitment to satisfy our own needs first so that we were in a better position to take care of others? That would be a radical reframe.

But most of the men I know who need to develop their Masculine core actually have the opposite problem. They don't know what they want, let alone share it. These are the nice guys who have fallen into the habit of hiding their needs just to get along. They feel like they're hurting others when they set a boundary, say "no", or ask for what they want.

But the opposite is true. The less you share your desires, the less others can feel who you really are and where you stand. You actually hurt people the most when you are not transparent with them.

Men who withhold their desires usually end up resorting to sneaky behaviors in order to covertly get their needs met. They manipulate to get what they want. They complain about not ever getting what they want, even while they rarely ask for it directly. Or they guilt and shame others into giving them what they want.

I have an example from my former marriage, though I'm not proud of it. It was in the phase where the children were very young. I would work all day, and then go to the company gym at around five o'clock. But I would tell my then-wife that I worked until 6 p.m., and not tell her I went to the gym. I did this because I knew she would not agree with this use of my time and would demand that I come home at five o'clock so I could help her with the kids. Instead of being transparent and assertive with my needs, I would covertly pursue what I wanted. When she eventually caught on, it was a major breach of trust for her that created more separation between us.

By far, **the most loving thing you can do for a partner or friend is to speak your truth about your needs and desires.** In the moment of choice when you are presented with an opportunity to either ignore or share your truth, remember this. Force yourself to live from that truth and have faith that the results will eventually be positive, even if there might be resistance or hurt feelings in the short term.

Without this capacity, you'll find yourself saying "*Yes*" to everyone else's needs. Inevitably, resentment will build up within you, and others will feel it. Your commitment to what you've agreed to may waver as a result, and you may become unreliable. People will start mistrusting your Yes and therefore mistrust your Masculine lead. If you want a Yes that people can trust, you need to first have a strong No.

Now, this is not guidance to simply become narcissistic, where your needs are the only ones that count. That's just being controlling. But many men are so far to the other end of the spectrum that this is not the greatest danger for them. They need to learn to be MORE selfish.

Repeat this mantra to yourself every day: **what I want matters**.

Make it your goal to regularly surface and state your desires clearly to others. Then use your discretion on how much to persist and insist after that. You will be amazed at the power that is created from simply having and stating what you're wanting or needing. In my own life, I've been amazed at how I encounter much less resistance to my desires than I thought simply by asking for them. **The more you own your desire, the more the universe will accommodate.**

In this state, you'll find yourself more relaxed and grounded. Instead of anxiously scanning everyone else to intuit or elicit their needs in order to make them happy, you'll be settled comfortably within yourself. You won't always get what you want, but you'll trust your desire and be willing to live with the consequences of your choices.

Of course, the shadow side of all of this is narcissism — you do what you want without regard to others. You have opinions about everything and steamroll others to get what you want. But true masculinity is not about dominating others without regard for their needs, but rather providing leadership and structure that incorporates their needs. Historically, a man could get away with being domineering. But today's capable women are not putting up with that nonsense if you aren't considering their needs as well. She's going to go straight into her own Masculine and resist you, which is, of course, the exact opposite of the Polarity you're trying to create. Balance your desire with the well-being of others.

CONCLUSION

Lose touch with your desires, needs, and boundaries at your own peril. It will kill Polarity in your relationship as your woman (or anyone else) fails to feel your Masculine clarity. Knowing what you want makes you sexy and more powerful in your woman's eyes. You're instantly going to stand out from the countless men throughout her life that didn't own what they wanted. While they were all scrambling around trying to manage her needs, you're just there powerfully grounded in your own.

CHAPTER 12

DIRECTION AND STRUCTURE

Life inherently involves navigating uncertainty and making decisions. Your woman naturally must go into her Masculine energy to deal with both of these things in much of her life. The more that you can reduce uncertainty, complexity, and the burden of decision making for your woman, the more she can relax. You do this by setting direction and providing structure — establishing processes and expectations, simplifying and driving decisions, setting boundaries, and clarifying communications.

If you're not doing this for the two of you, she'll either have to step in and do it herself or prod *you* into doing it. To you that will feel like she's nagging and being bossy. To her, it is just a bid for your leadership.

THE GIFT OF THE MASCULINE

The notion that you would be the one to provide structure may seem like controversial advice because many will interpret it to mean that you're supposed to be in charge and your woman should be subservient to you. That is NOT what we're talking about here.

The truth is that your woman can probably make most of her own decisions and work out most situations in her life. Some things will be natural, and others will be harder, but she'll figure it out. However, she doesn't want to *have* to do this. At least not all of the time.

Uncertainty and decision making require her to go into her Masculine energy. Obviously, you're interested in getting her OUT of her Masculine and back into the Feminine energy you so enjoy. So when you take the lead, she can relax and flow within the direction and structure that you create.

This is not about being domineering. It is not you controlling her or doubting her abilities. On the contrary, I am talking about offering structure and direction as a GIFT to your woman to temporarily relieve her of this burden.

It is, of course, a paradox. Women have fought and continue to fight to gain equality with men. It may be hard to reconcile this drive for equality with the notion that I'm presenting. But that is part of the art of Masculine leadership — knowing how to lead while still allowing for your woman's capability, power, and equality. You invite her to follow your lead, she chooses whether to take it.

Tango works the same way. It is a strong lead-follow dance, but you do not <u>force</u> her body to go where you want. Rather, a good lead will use his body to signal an invitation for her to move in a certain way. He signals, then waits and listens for her bodily response. A skilled lead never forces. He invites, and lets her acceptance unfold as it will. This is the style of Masculine leadership that you can provide to your woman.

Unfortunately, men have forgotten how to lead. We've become passive, afraid to take risks. Afraid to say or do the wrong thing. We poke around and see what our woman wants or wants us to do, then do it. Too many men have forgotten how to be bold with their woman and simply initiate a direction.

So if you want to put your woman more into her Feminine, stop waiting for clues or orders from her. Just step up and be proactive. The first and most straightforward way you can do this is to set direction for the two of you.

SETTING DIRECTION

We all know that making decisions in life can be tiring. You have to gather all the available information, factor in uncertainty, synthesize it all, make a decision, and take action. If others are involved, you have to make accommodations for their needs and preferences. And you risk their disapproval of your decision. We all may claim to want sovereignty in life, but once in a while it is nice when someone else just makes the decision for us.

But if you want to invite your woman into her Feminine, YOU need to take this on. Bringing Masculine clarity and direction alleviates her from having to do it herself. You have to take the lead in driving decisions.

This doesn't mean you MAKE all of the decisions. It means that **you make sure a decision gets made, whether or not you're actually deciding**. You are proactive in identifying that a decision needs to be made, gathering enough information to form your own opinion or proposal, and then either making the decision or putting it on the table for the two of you to make.

What the Masculine doesn't do is ignore the decision, pontificate about it, or wait for someone else to make it.

I remember a situation with a group of my old friends trying to set up a reunion weekend. The discussion went round and round endlessly on email about possible dates and locations. At some point, two of us had hit our limit with the never-ending debate, so we just chose the best date possible and a specific city, and put it out there as "the" plan. Not surprisingly, we settled on things very quickly and eight of the ten guys were able to attend. All it took was someone to step up and make a decision for the group. It wasn't democratic, but it moved us forward.

You can choose to set direction as a gift to your woman. Examples of this can range from the tactical to the strategic:

- Driving a decision on where to go to dinner or take your next vacation. You choose a few candidates and do research on their characteristics, cost, and availability. Then share with her one, two, or three options, and ask her opinion.
- Having a clear opinion on how to handle a child-raising situation that has arisen. It is an exercise in researching options, then looking within to see which of them feels right for your parenting style and values, as well as feasibility.
- Mapping out a plan for the day's trip to the beach that you agreed to take. Research traffic patterns, parking, and where to rent wetsuits. Give her a target departure time, and start identifying and packing up some of the basic supplies you'll need.
- Researching and proposing specific investments for your joint money to prepare for your eventual retirement together. You also run the numbers on how much you need to be saving and determine the budget you need to stay within.

In these examples, you're not leaving situations ignored or on auto-pilot until she's forced to bring them up or do something about them. You're being proactive in addressing them.

And you're NOT asking her what she wants and just giving it to her in order to make her happy. That won't create Polarity. What you are doing is taking on the prep work of synthesizing all the information necessary to make the decision. You're simplifying uncertainty.

You can then offer this in a multitude of ways. Some situations might dictate that you call the ball and declare *"Here's what we're doing."* You do this not out of domineering ego, but rather because you know this is what is best for the both of you in this particular moment. She may be caught in such a cycle of neurosis or indecision that she will be served best by your firm guidance in the situation. This recently happened for me when my woman wanted to go out for a glass of wine after our hike instead of heading home to finish up the paperwork for an insurance filing she needed to complete, as we'd planned. She first asked my opinion *"Should we go home or go get a glass of wine?"* I said we should go home so she could get her paperwork done. She started to insist on going out, and got a little pushy about it. But I knew deep down that this was just an avoidance pattern on her part. I put my hands on her shoulders and said: *"Darling, we're going home now, end of story."* She grumbled for a few minutes until coming around and thanking me for keeping her on track.

Once in a while, your woman wants you to just say *"Babe, put on that red dress I like, I'm taking you out!"* You don't even need to tell her the place if you'd like to keep a little mystery going. **This level of direction and clarity can be like catnip to the Feminine psyche.** Your woman will love being on your ride, and love relaxing into your direction.

And, you'll need to be able to do this even when tensions are high. One of my clients did a great job of this in such a situation:

Dan and Jen were walking to dinner and out of the blue things got a little tense. Jen was a little triggered from something that had happened to her earlier in the day, unrelated to Dan. So she was a little grouchy and he got a little reactive and defensive. On the walk back from dinner, they were only able to half-process things, so each was still feeling a bit shut down. They did not live together and had taken separate cars that night to meet downtown for dinner right after work. Because things had gotten prickly, Dan felt the overwhelming urge to just go home to his own house and be alone rather than stay over at Jen's as previously planned. But his instinct told him not to go down that road. That it would be running away rather than leading. The issue would only get calcified and harder to resolve later. Then Jen said "Maybe we should just be apart tonight," and in that moment Dan made the instant choice to step into a leadership role rather than turn away from the anxiety that this fight was producing inside of him: "No, we're not going to do that. It will only bury the issues. Let's drive to your place and get in bed, and you can say anything more you need to say then." She instantly felt his leadership, and simply said "OK". They drove back to her house, and things had settled. They were able to quickly process the remaining feelings. They made love that night and woke up feeling connected.

I was proud of Dan. Our work together was paying off in how he was showing up as a leader in his relationship. He could have easily chosen the path of being separate that night, but that would have had long-term negative impact. Unaddressed issues turn into sediment, and over the years layers and layers get built up. Eventually, you can neither feel each other nor dig through the long-hardened sediment. Dan made sure that didn't happen by making a hard decision for the two of them. He led them out of a bad place.

And, while it is good that you can take charge once in a while, in the majority of situations you can simply offer your direction as a proposal: "*Baby, here's what I think is best. How does that feel to you?*" You're not pushing a decision onto her, but you've done the legwork to frame the decision and offer an opinion. This still relieves her of much of the full burden of making a decision.

An effective approach for doing this is to whittle down the uncertainty and narrow the scope for your woman. Anything to avoid just lobbing a wide open decision at her ("*What do YOU want to do?*"). Let's take a look at a few ways you might do this using the simple example of choosing a place to eat:

> **Ask for any objection**: "*Babe, I'm thinking of Mexican at the place on Polk Street, or Sushi at our favorite place on Columbus. Would you object to either of those?*" You've narrowed the options to two and are giving her the option to express objections to one or both.

> **Present options**: "*Babe, I would be up for Mexican, Sushi, or Italian. Which one sounds best to you?*" You are asking her to make a decision, but you've significantly narrowed the choices she has to consider.

> **Express a preference**: "*I would love to go to Mexican, but I'm open to other options.*" Expressing your preference

gives her something specific to which to respond, which simplifies things for her.

Express what you don't want*: "Babe, I'm open to anything to eat tonight, but not Italian, Sushi, and Mexican." Again, you're limiting the scope of the decision, in this case by sharing what you DON'T want to do.*

In each case, you've simplified the decision while still offering her a chance to participate. Every one of these options is better than just a lame *"I don't know, what do you want to eat tonight?"* **You are always moving the process forward, balancing inclusiveness with decisiveness and progress.**

Never underestimate the simple power of temporarily relieving her of decision-making burden. Trust me, this sounds simple, but works like magic.

• • •

And, in contrast, there will also be times when you are actually far less capable than her to take the lead in certain domains. In an earlier chapter, I gave the example of cooking with my woman, a domain in which I am not competent. I shared that my technique is to say *"Baby, tell me what to do."* I am still setting direction by being clear that she needs to guide me in the kitchen. This removes the uncertainty about what each of us are doing in this joint cooking venture. This will relax her. You don't need to be "in charge" in order to set direction.

There are also going to be decisions about which you simply don't care. Maybe the color of the drapes in the living room, or the types of flowers at your wedding. She may ask you for your opinion, and your instinct may be to say *"I don't care, this is not my domain, whatever you want."* I advise you to actually form an opinion. Her question was a bid for your clarity. She may be just a little unsure of her own opinion and needs yours to get her over the tipping point of her uncertainty. This is a bid to feel the "we" rather than feeling like she's on her own to make the decision. Don't let it go unanswered. Have an opinion, even if you *think* you don't care.

Finally, remember that setting direction needs to extend beyond just the initial decision about what to do. Using the example from above, once you've chosen the restaurant, there is still more direction for you to provide: making the reservation, knowing how long it will take to drive there and therefore what time to leave, knowing where to park safely, telling her the temperature so she dresses appropriately, and bringing an umbrella if needed. The more you can bring leadership and simplification to all of the elements of the activity, the more relaxed she will be.

STRUCTURE IN THE "HOW"

Setting direction and driving decisions is how you provide structure for WHAT you'll do. But you can also provide structure in HOW you'll do things. The distinction is not a strict one, but it holds up for purposes of us exploring it here.

One way to do this is by establishing the rules of engagement for how the two of you will handle conflict (I've heard this called "establishing the culture of the relationship"). It could sound like: *"Baby, it is non-negotiable for me that we never go to sleep mad at each other and disconnected. When we fight, we will stay up until we can at least re-establish connection, even if we don't get it all figured out. This is very important to me. Can you commit to this?"* You're not trying to dictate or dominate the content of any particular fight. Rather, you're taking a hard line on the container within which you'll fight.

I had a recent example of this in my life. My woman and I had an argument and were both feeling rather shut down. It lingered into the next day, so I proposed that both of us write down five things that we appreciate about each other, and then go on a walk and read them to each other. Without taking on the content of the argument directly (which was feeling impossible in the moment), we tapped into our deeper appreciation of each other. It softened both of us. And it was my offering of this structure that helped lead us out of the feeling of shutdown and enabled us to eventually address the original issue.

You can also offer structure in ways not necessarily related to relational conflict, such as in these examples:

- Insist on a regular practice of sitting down to coordinate your schedules for the upcoming day, week, month, or year. This kind of exercise reduces her uncertainty about your joint and individual plans. You're creating a structure to facilitate this.

- Create a norm of once a month having a heart-to-heart discussion about your relationship and anything you need to clear with each other. Her nervous system will relax knowing that the two of you have this regular forum in which you can emotionally heal and connect. You've created structure that makes this kind of repair work a regular and predictable event.

- Overcommunicate about all kinds of logistics in your life. This could mean responding quickly to her questions and comments over text (even if only to acknowledge receipt) so she is not left in a state of suspense. Or, it might mean circling back to reiterate or confirm a plan you've previously discussed, just to ensure there is no confusion. By consistently and predictably doing these things, you're creating structure in your communications which helps avoid miscommunication and uncertainty.

- Before asking her about her opinion or needs, share yours first. This allows her to understand your orientation first before sharing hers. It frees her from wondering where you stand, and gives her something around which to orient her own thinking before answering. It will settle her nervous system.

- When you know she has a hard task to complete, get her to agree to a scheduled time in which you'll both sit down and you will help her get it done. You've created structure within which she is forced to confront her difficult tasks but knows she'll be getting support from you.

- Insist on and plan out regular date night where you do something new and interesting (dinner and a movie won't cut it).

- Choose the music to specifically fit the mood. Energy in the morning, background during focus time, and something sensual in the bedroom.

A friend of mine did an admirable job of providing structure for his woman in a way similar to the last bullet above:

> *Mathias and Karen had just moved in together, and she was beginning to feel overwhelmed with the number of decisions to make about which of their stuff to keep and which to get rid of (their place was small). Her feeling of overwhelm turned into an acute bad mood and she started lashing out at him. Mathias took decisive action by asking her to sit down and then bringing her kitchen items from which to choose. He brought out the three colanders that they owned between the two of them, and told her*

she could keep one. Karen chose one and he put the other two out in the garage. Then he moved to mixing bowls, then wooden spoons, then measuring cups, and so forth. Sometimes she tried to keep two and he pushed back. If she persisted, he'd say "OK, you can keep two for sixty days, but after that, we will reevaluate and see if you really need them both."

At each step, he was doing an amazing job of providing structure for her, while giving ground at the right times in order to accommodate her needs.

And at no point did he steamroll her. Rather, he just provided structure and helped her through a task that was proving very difficult for her. She later reported that she felt an enormous sense of relief because of it.

WHY DON'T MEN DO THIS?

A reasonable question to ask is: if the benefits of providing direction and structure are so self-evident, then why don't all men do it? There are a variety of reasons, and I'll address a few here.

Some men simply have no connection to their own desires and needs. We discussed this at length in the last chapter. Without knowing what you want, there is no anchor from which to set direction. The only thing you can do is figure out what SHE wants and give it to her. That is not setting direction — it's following direction.

Other men may simply be pleasers, and the notion of asserting themselves in the relationship like we've discussed is out of the question. Pleasers cannot set direction. They're too scared to go out on a limb and own what they want.

Many modern men play life with too much egalitarianism. They believe that intimate relationship is a partnership of equals in all things. Therefore, every decision is a joint decision preceded by a joint discussion of views. It doesn't even occur to them that they can take the lead and initiate a direction.

Believe it or not, there are also some men are just too lazy to take the lead. Making decisions, holding structures, and moving things forward are rather time-consuming, exhausting activities. It's just too hard. For them, it is much easier to just abdicate.

There are other men who are simply so busy that they see this aspect of Masculine leadership as a burden. It is not that they are unwilling to do it, but rather that they feel too busy to take it on. I must admit that I suffered from this orientation in my marriage. I was so busy working and helping raise the kids that I didn't step fully into a leadership role. As a result, my partner did not always experience me as a leader, which pushed her into her own Masculine. So I encourage you not to see it as a burden, but rather a choice. You either choose to give this gift, or you don't. But don't make excuses about it being a burden on your time. It is too important to be dismissed like that.

And finally, a man might not set direction and structure because he tried it a few times early on and his woman resisted vociferously. It ended up feeling like it would be a lot of work to fight through her resistance, and it began to feel a bit hopeless that she'd ever follow his lead. Worse, his male ego may have gotten bruised by her pushback, and so he stopped asserting himself in order to avoid what felt like rejection.

I know a man who has been married for over twenty-five years to the same woman. When I asked him why he never seemed to take the lead with his wife (and why he also seemed subtly but clearly angry with her), he eventually confided in me that he'd tried that in the first couple of years after they got married, but she never would yield to his lead. So he just quit trying. And for twenty-five years he lived as a limp but secretly angry husband.

So as you now attempt to step into this role in your own relationship, remember a few things. First, don't take any pushback from her personally. It's natural that she initially won't trust your leadership after years of you being passive. You just need to gently persist. Second, remember that she has wisdom as well, and you need to learn the art of weaving it in. If you are disregarding it, she'll resist. And third, remember that her willingness to accept your direction will ebb and flow. Read the situation, and modulate between gentle guidance and strong direction based on how open she is to your lead. I guarantee that the more connected the two of you are, the more open she'll be to your lead.

And, most importantly, if she's resisting your leadership, don't try to steamroll her, i.e. the proverbial *"I have spoken, and this is how it's going to be, woman!"* Don't even think about that. Rather than a bullrush in response to her resistance, use your discretion about whether to gently but firmly persist because it is token resistance (as in the example I gave earlier about the glass of wine after the hike), or to back off and check in with her about her needs.

CLARITY IS KEY

I've said before that being certain and clear is the foundation of setting direction and providing structure. But I've heard a lot of men express that they simply don't experience high levels of clarity in their lives. Often, they'll claim to be "easy-going guys", who view their own lack of strong preferences as a virtue. Others tell me that they may have opinions but get steamrolled by their woman, who always seems to have incredibly strong opinions about many topics. So they just yield to her.

I encourage you to NOT to get caught in either of these traps.

There is no silver bullet. But clarity starts with simply giving yourself permission to listen to that quiet voice inside of you that knows what you prefer and what you think is the best way forward. Give yourself permission to have your own voice in any situation. Listen to and nurture that voice. **Develop the rock-solid belief that your opinions matter and that your wisdom is sound**.

Tap deeply into your beliefs, values, mission, instincts, the way you want to be treated, how you want to spend your time, etc. Make it a practice to learn to LISTEN to the gut reactions they create within you.

Give yourself permission to act on your gut reactions. Stop trying to over-optimize and overthink in order to find the perfect solution. Go with your instincts more often, without feeling the need to always defend your choices.

And most of all, simply start developing the muscle of CHOOSING. You can build it up. Tend toward less seeking of permission and more doing. **Make mistakes of action rather than inaction**. Just make decisions, and you'll gain confidence as you go.

All of this may sound like simply positive thinking to you. But it is far more than that.

First, you are rewiring your brain to accept that you have needs and preferences, that you deserve to have them met, and that you can use them to lead others.

Second, it is strengthening your nervous system to handle the natural fear that comes up for most of us around knowing what we want, pursuing it, and leading others toward it. In taking charge, you risk others' anger and rejection. This book is about training your nervous system to get past this fear.

CONCLUSION

Women wanted men to be less domineering and more sensitive to their needs and capabilities. We responded by becoming afraid to lead. Afraid to give our women the gift of our Masculine clarity.

Don't stop giving this gift. Don't step into the backseat in order to avoid her displeasure. Your woman still wants your leadership.

She wants you to step in and provide direction and structure in the places where she's not as strong or clear herself. And where she's strong, she still wants your facilitation of a decision that folds in her wisdom, needs, and input. Without bullying her into anything, she wants you to lead. Do that, and your woman will feel well taken care of.

CHAPTER 13

SEXUAL LEADERSHIP

Men who don't bring their Masculine leadership will find their woman becoming increasingly irritable, closed, and challenging over time. This is most true in the sexual domain, where your woman absolutely wants you to lead her into her pleasure. She craves to be able to relax into your direction in the bedroom.

WHY SHE SHUTS DOWN SEXUALLY

There will be times when your woman is not feeling sexual at all due to the stresses of life and relationship. A true Masculine leader can often skillfully lead her out of that state into her sexuality.

So if you find yourself in a situation with your woman not feeling sexual, don't complain. Don't wait for her to change. Don't just buy her flowers to curry favor with her. Don't fall back on the excuse that she's become frigid.

No, don't do any of these things. Instead, accept the fact that it's your job to LEAD her back into her sexuality (assuming consent, of course). You CAN help her find that part of herself again.

Never assume that her shutting down sexually is "just the way things are". There IS a reason she's feeling that way. You might consider two common possibilities.

1. She's not feeling loved and led. In this state, her heart starts to close and her body quickly follows. Unlike men, women need safety and heart connection to feel sexual. **When you're chronically defensive, unempathetic, indecisive, overly pleasing, nice, unreliable, or anxious, she's not going to feel loved and led.** And therefore she likely won't open her body to you.

2. She's tired of your unskillful sex. **Never confuse a woman who's not interested in sex with one who is not interested in the sex that's available to her.** She was likely a sexual being when you met her. She probably still is, but may not like what you've been bringing. This happens when you haven't made the effort to develop your sexual skills, to know how to properly warm her up and turn her on.

It's common for both of these situations to exist in established relationships. And they make her body close, which causes her to reject your advances. This leaves you feeling unworthy, ashamed, and probably angry — all perfectly natural responses in this situation. Men have a deep need to feel like they can turn their women on. Her arousal feels like a validation of your virility and worth. In contrast, **her disinterest in sex feels like a rejection of YOU as a person.** This is painful.

Sadly, I can speak from experience here. By the end of my marriage, sex was non-existent. I remember seeing a news article back then about "Low Sex Marriages". The article said that this label applied if sex was once a month. I recall thinking to myself: "*Wow, once a month. That actually sounds pretty good!*" I laugh about it now, but back then it was not so funny. My wife at the time was so closed to me that sex was not happening. My ego suffered greatly, and I saw no way out of it

I am here to tell you, very clearly: you CAN change the situation. You CAN learn how to open your woman up. You CAN awaken her into a level of sexual interest that you remember from when you first met, and go way beyond it.

You do this by loving and leading her outside the bedroom, as we've been discussing all along.

And you do this by bringing your Masculine leadership into the bedroom. By becoming more grounded, setting direction, and creating safety, you CAN open her up.

And this is true whether she's just feeling shut down in the moment, or has been chronically shut down for days, months, or years. You can almost always affect the situation to some degree.

I am a firm believer that both partners have a right to expect a healthy sex life. If either person's interest unilaterally wanes, and the other is chronically left wanting, that's not OK. Do NOT settle for a sexless relationship (except, of course, in cases of some type of health impairment). Do not even settle for a *low* sex relationship. Life is short. There is too much fun and pleasure to be experienced with your woman to tolerate a situation like this over the long term.

So, if your relationship has less sex than you want, do something about it. Stop waiting for her. Stop being tentative. Open your woman up by *leading* her into her sexuality.

HOW TO LEAD HER

Doing this is not easy, but may be more straightforward than you think. Here is a very simple reality: women in relationship tend to more easily open up sexually when a) the conditions exist for them to feel safe and b) when they're warmed up slowly. It is really that simple. When you take the lead in putting those conditions in place and warming her up slowly, she's much more likely to open sexually (again, barring certain factors such as a medical condition or a state of chronic disconnection).

In fact, the process I've just described has a name that I know you've heard before: seduction. You do very specific things to tempt and draw her into a state of turn on. I'll admit that when I used to hear the word seduction, I'd think of some romantic wannabe serenading his woman, or a pickup artist trying to work his manipulations. I did not think of it as a core component of Masculine leadership. But it is.

In contrast, the opposite of seduction is the assumption that she gets instantly turned on like you and your male physiology do, such as when you fall into bed after a long day and then try to grope her without first bringing her into her body. Or, it could look like you trying to initiate sex without having established a heart connection with her throughout the day. Both approaches are naive. And it's agonizing to your woman.

News flash: your woman is DYING for you to seduce her.

And, believe it or not, seduction is easier than you think. Know what you want and what feels good to her. Know how to do it. And then bravely do it. That's it.

"Knowing what you want" is nothing more than having a sense of what turns you on and what turns her on. See Chapter 11.

"Knowing how to do it" means becoming a student of sexuality and developing skills from the many resources out there. It also means learning about your woman's body. Be proactive and dedicate the time to get smarter.

"Bravely doing it" means having the courage to initiate sexual experiences with your woman, despite any shame you have around sexuality or hesitation because of prior rejection. Take charge.

Many men struggle with this last one. Society has conditioned you to be democratic and egalitarian with your woman. Taking charge, even dominating her, feels a bit forbidden. But sexuality over the long term in a relationship requires this at times. As David Deida says: "*You need a ravisher and a ravishee.*" You need a Masculine pole and a Feminine pole. You need someone to lead, and someone to surrender. So lead her, trust your instincts, take some risks, and don't look for pre-approval on every little thing (within the bounds of consent, of course).

It is fear, shame, and lack of skill that hold you back. All create anxiety in you. And all are absolutely addressable. Make a commitment to yourself that starting today, you'll create change around sex in your relationship.

Educate yourself and improve your sexual skills. Leverage the many instructional resources out there (that are not porn). Having more skill will reduce your anxiety, make you more grounded, and support your courage to lead. Exposure to these resources will also help reduce your sexual shame because they can help normalize healthy sexual expression.

Your sexual leadership is an extension of the work I'm sharing in this book around developing your Masculine core and increasing your nervous system's capacity for the intensity and anxiety. When you're grounded in your Masculine core, you will be more fearless in leading your woman to her pleasure.

• • •

Now, let's return to what I said earlier about seduction: women open up sexually to their man more when a) the conditions exist for them to feel safe, and b) when they're warmed up slowly. I will now spend time discussing each of these separately.

CREATING THE CONTAINER

The Masculine leader provides structure, and in the sexual domain this manifests as you **creating a "container" in which your woman's Feminine sexual energy can flourish**. The "conditions" I mentioned earlier are what create the "container". They create a sense of safety within which she can relax and open up into her sexuality. Maybe even go wild.

Below, I will share with you eight conditions which help create this container for her: Timing, Environment, Heart Connection, Presence, Praise, Owning Sexuality, Edginess, and Attunement.

We start with **Timing**. One way you can provide structure for her is to manage the timing of your sexuality, because in her turned on state she's going to lose all sense of time.

If the sex is spontaneous, you need to be aware of the time duration of your play so that you don't inadvertently make either of you late for any obligations. She's going to be upset with you if you tempt her into sexuality and then she is late for an appointment, or if the plumber rings the doorbell while the two of you are in the throes of passion. She'll feel like you didn't set a container around time, and going forward she'll think that she has to be the one to track it since you didn't. She won't fully relax if she's having to track time. But if she knows you're tracking, then she *can* relax.

One way I like to handle this is simply to inquire about my woman's obligations or availability and then set a timer. This creates the time container. It is a simple thing to do to pause briefly and communicate about time, even in the midst of spontaneity. It need not spoil the mood and will pay dividends in her opening up to you.

You can also create structure around time by consciously scheduling sexual "dates" with your woman. Take the initiative to propose a specific time for the two of you to be intimate. It's like asking her on a date. Creating this structure around time and intention gives her the opportunity to take care of her worldly business and get herself into a state of mind for sexuality.

I used to have an unconscious bias that scheduling like this made sex a little too *planned*. I've since loosened up around this belief. Setting sexuality dates with my woman has proven very successful in leading to MORE sex. It's very simple. If I know my woman has some things to get done before she'll relax, I'll say *"Baby, how about we both get our own stuff done this morning and then get in bed together at 1 p.m.?"*

· · ·

The next condition is **Environment**. Women are very sensitive to their environment, and never more than when being sexual. Opening their body requires a requisite level of beauty and comfort in their surroundings. This is usually not a man's forte. So, I offer these following tips.

Make sure the room temperature is warm enough. If you're going to hide under the covers, then this is less important. But that's pretty limiting to your sexual range. Covers make it difficult to see her naked body. Covers make it difficult to have her legs spread out straight up in the air. Covers are suffocating on your head when you're going down on her. And covers don't work very well with her on all fours. Yet in the heat of passion, if you try to do any of these things (which I hope you do because it means you're initiating variety) and pull the covers off of her, she's going to get cold, feel unsafe, and start to pull back bodily. Think ahead.

Pay attention to the lighting. It can make a big difference to the experience. It sets the mood. If you're smart, you'll use candles as they provide a great hue of light, and their flicker creates dynamism. Candles are also usually dim enough to help hide the bodily flaws that all of us stress over, particularly women. She will feel less self-conscious about her body, and thus relax and open up a bit more.

Music also creates mood, so choose wisely. Personally, I recommend against jarring playlists of rock or rap, as well as too-obviously sexual tracks like Marvin Gaye's "Let's Get It On". Find what meets your woman's tastes and will soothe her nerves. But maintain variety as well — you don't want to create a "standard" playlist that gets too strongly associated with sexuality. The Feminine psyche will begin to experience this as forced-Pavlovian, as if she's supposed to perform when you play THAT music. It can make sexuality feel a bit obligatory to her.

Good sex often includes tools of pleasure: a vibrator, lube, condoms, toys, etc. You don't want to break the flow of things to go find them when needed. Part of your container is to have these items set out near your area of play for easy access. Some of my clients have resisted this notion because they said it looks too presumptuous or pre-planned. I say it is better to be ready and allow for the full range of sexuality rather than interrupt the action because you don't have the right tools easily available.

• • •

Next, we consider **Heart Connection**. Most women desire or require some requisite level of emotional connection with you before opening sexually. A woman's yoni is wired directly to her heart. When she feels love flowing, her heart opens. And only then does her body truly open to you.

So, if she's not feeling connected to you, she isn't going to be in a sexual state of mind. Don't make the mistake of projecting onto her the male paradigm of sexuality in which you can get turned on instantly, no matter the state of connection between you. Men will settle for sex as an activity of physical release ("scratch-the-itch" sex, usually orgasm focused) for which they are perpetually ready. But most women see sex as an act of emotional/physical union, one which requires emotional connection and resonance with their partners.

What puts her in this state? All of the things we've been discussing in this book. At the highest level, it is feeling loved and led by you. Feeling loved means you being in your heart and sharing it with her. It means her feeling connected to you, and you taking care of her. Feeling lcd means you staying grounded, providing structure, and making her feel safe in all the ways previously discussed.

So if you are not feeling her open up sexually, then pause and try to re-establish connection first. This could be as easy as doing an eye gazing and breathing exercise. Or it could be more involved, such as going through a process of proactively addressing any unresolved issues between the two of you.

If there is a chronic level of disconnection between the two of you, don't be surprised if she is chronically shut down to sex. It will require a long road to excavate the sediment that has built up between the two of you. She needs to be clear of resentments to really open up her body. But it can be done through the consistent application of what I'm sharing in this book.

• • •

The next condition is **Presence**. In order to open sexually, your woman needs you to be fully here, in the now. Below are a few tips I offer in this vein.

First, turn off your phone. You don't need the distraction of a ringer or the ding of a text message to draw your attention away from her. We are all so tuned to immediately respond to our phone's notifications in Pavlovian fashion. It controls us, often without us realizing it. But SHE notices your distraction. It feels like a dagger in her heart.

Presence also manifests in eye contact, which is one of the best and easiest ways to create connection in the moment. It is very erotic, but most people avoid it during sexuality. I've had experiences of lovers who averted their gaze while being intimate, and I found that it negatively impacted my turn on. Imagine how painful it is for your woman, whose Feminine nature craves connection, if you don't hold eye contact. And if she is not initiating, make a very direct request of her to join you in it.

Presence in sex also entails being verbally communicative. Some people simply go mute during sexuality because of shyness or shame. But verbal communications can help the two of you feel closer. It may be whispering sweet nothings, talking dirty, or checking in with her on whether something you're doing feels good. The caveat is that communications only pertain to the present moment. Absolutely no talk about "real world" topics — it will put both of you into your heads instantly. Save that for later.

Further, this prohibition against real-life logistical talk can extend to the time leading up to sex. My woman and I recently had planned to get into bed for an early evening delight after a day of skiing. But we needed to shower first. While we were both in the bathroom getting ready, I noticed the natural urge to have regular conversation. But it occurred to me in that moment that regular conversation is rather de-polarizing. It puts you in a collaborative mode, like two good friends rather than lovers who are about to be ravisher and ravishee. I realized in that moment that it was simply better not to talk at all because it would negatively affect the Polarity. So I made that request of my woman, who saw the wisdom and readily agreed. We stayed silent until we got into bed and managed to maintain the Polarity.

●   ●   ●

Let us now look at **Praise**. You're seeking to set up conditions that open your woman up and draw her into her sexuality. Praise can do that. This may seem counterintuitive, so let me explain how.

David Deida says that just like a man's deepest desire is to be trusted by his woman, an important need of the Feminine is to feel desirable. Your praise of her beauty is deeply pleasurable to her. "*You are so beautiful*" or something like "*I love seeing you naked.*" And, as your woman gets older or has gotten a bit out of shape, I encourage you to FIND the beauty in her. Find something in her that you can acknowledge as beautiful, whether it be physical or energetic.

Expressing your desire for her is also a form of praise. "*I can't wait to get your clothes off*" or "*I'm going to devour you*" are great examples. To feel desired is intoxicating to the Feminine, and your expression will go a long way in opening her up in this way.

Praise can also be used as a way to encourage certain behavior, rather than asking for it explicitly or complaining about a lack. If you were to say "*I wish you would go down on me more,*" her Feminine nature will experience that as criticism, which won't open her. Instead, you might use praise: "*I love when you go down on me. It feels so good.*" The Feminine will better respond to this approach.

I will share one specific way I've used this in my relationship. Over time, I began to realize that when my woman is bodily or verbally responsive during sexuality, it is a huge turn on for me. I want more of it because that responsiveness sets up a circuit of energy between us: I pleasure her, she expresses that pleasure bodily or through vocalization, I subsequently get more turned on, which then turns her on more. Her overt expressiveness created this circuit. But I know if I explicitly ask for it, she might resist because it could possibly feel like an obligation. So, I choose to praise her. Both in and out of sexual situations, I express how much I enjoy her responsiveness, and how much it turns me on. Over time, she's become more and more overtly responsive as a result of my praise. I encourage you to learn to use it yourself to influence your woman for the better. The Feminine loves praise.

• • •

The next condition is to **Own Your Sexuality**. It is critical to create a container in which sexual shame does not exist. And if you're feeling any shame, it can cause closure in her. Likewise, the more you unabashedly own your sexuality, the more of an uninhibited sex kitten she will become.

This may not be natural for you. Certainly, most American men tend to keep their sexuality hidden, an artifact of the country's puritanical roots where sex was considered by prior generations to be dirty and needed to be concealed.

The impact of this shame is tangible. You don't make eye contact during sex. You are afraid to share your fantasies with your lover, or ask for what you want. You're afraid to offer any dirty talk. In other words, you stay safe and vanilla.

If you have a knot in your gut thinking about this, don't worry. You're not alone, and it is something you can grow past. Below I offer some suggestions.

First, start to expose yourself to more intentional sexuality. I don't mean porn. You probably get enough of that. I mean real-world experiences and training. Read educational books on healthy but edgy sexuality. Take a class on rope bondage. Do a weekend workshop on intimacy, or even BDSM. Hire a sexuality coach. All of these things are available to help you expand your sexual boundaries. What you will find are people who think and talk about sex very openly. They experiment, play, and explore without shame. This path of exploration will expand your range and reduce your own shame around sex.

Never desexualize yourself with your woman. Don't deny that you want sex, or obfuscate your pursuit of it. I recall a client who told me a story about a situation like this:

> *Mick had just finished a full weekend day of cleaning out the garage. He knew that his wife Kat had started to get annoyed about how cluttered it had been. He admitted that he'd wanted to make her happy because they hadn't been sexual in weeks. But when he got done, she sarcastically said: "Oh, I see someone is trying to earn some sex for himself." To which he quickly and defensively said "No, no! It's not like that at all." Which, of course, was completely untrue.*

Mick was suffering from the lack of sex, but instead of owning his natural need for intimacy with her, Mick went about it sideways. He tried to do things to make his wife happy so that she'd be more open to sex. And, he DENIED it being about sex when she asked. Because of his own embedded shame, he was unable to be transparent about his sexual needs.

This is a pervasive problem for men. Just like any of the non-Masculine behaviors we've discussed in this book, it is the anxiety created by shame which will hold you back from fully owning your sexuality. Standing in front of your woman, it is that moment of decision — do you admit your turn on, ask for a specific sexual act, invite her into sexual play, command her, say something dirty, give her a playful spanking, or admit a dark fantasy to her? It is in that moment that anxiety grips most men and prevents them from expressing or acting.

I can empathize because I was like that fifteen years ago until I started to access the myriad of resources available to expand my own boundaries (it helps to live in San Francisco). I tell you this to help you believe that it CAN be different for you if you take steps to expand your boundaries.

• • •

The next condition is, ironically, **Edginess**. Although you always want to be creating safety for your woman, you don't want it to be *too* safe. If sex is always safe, it becomes boring. If you're always gentle, supportive, heart-centered, and nice in sex, you become boring. Boredom is a strong headwind to her opening up as your wild little sex kitten.

So, keep it a little edgy. Some suggested ways:

- Don't smile in sex too much. My woman once told me she could never surrender to a man who smiled during sex. Past lovers who did that felt to her that they were trying to be nice, when she was actually craving their intensity and dominance. Try powerful eye contact rather than a smile.
- Some dirty talk can be very effective in creating sexual tension. We'll discuss this more below.
- Don't be afraid to command her. So many women are longing for their man to be dominant once in a while.
- Suspense can feel playfully edgy. Cover her eyes, or move slowly with long pauses to keep her guessing as to what you'll do next.
- Intermix forcefulness with your slow control. Below we'll discuss the power of moving slowly. But don't forget to surprise her with an occasional quick movement of her body. When you're standing there kissing her, you might quickly (but carefully) spin her

around 180 degrees, wrap your arms around her while pinning hers to her sides, and start playfully nibbling on her neck.

- Consensual impact or restraint play (discussed below) can add an edge to your sexuality. Give her a little spanking or pin her arms behind her back.

Your art is to blend safety with edginess in your sexuality. Don't make the mistake of avoiding sexual tension and skipping straight to comfort. Sexual tension is absolutely necessary to keep the fire alive in your woman. It is part of the container, albeit an ironic one, that will serve to open her up.

• • •

Now, the final condition is **Attunement**. Your woman needs to feel that you're tuned in to her needs and her body rather than being lost in your own sensation during sexuality. If you're making love, and something is not feeling quite right to her, she wants to know that you're paying attention, you will notice, and you'll make a course correction. Otherwise, it feels like you're on autopilot. And that is a lonely feeling for her.

Gentlemen, learn to attune to your woman's state. It starts with you being fully present. Visually track how her body responds and the subtle facial expressions that will tell you if she's enjoying what you're doing to her. Have fifty percent of your attention on your own sensation, of course, but reserve fifty percent for watching and sensing into her responses. If she moans or her eyes roll back in her head, for instance, then keep doing what you're doing. If she stops breathing or furrows her brow, then you should be sensing that and adjusting. Sense and adjust. Sense and adjust. Even if she's not speaking the words, her body is giving you all kinds of signals which tell you "*That's it*" or "*I'm not liking that.*"

It is fine if you need to occasionally ask "*How does that feel, Love?*" if she's not giving overt signals and you need to check in. **But be careful to not overuse the inquiry**. It can give the impression that you don't know what you're doing or that you're asking permission for everything you do to her. It also puts her into her thinking mind having to evaluate and respond to each inquiry. Be judicious.

Now, as you attune to her, **you must be open to her expressing that something *doesn't* feel good**. Unfortunately, men too often take this as a rejection and start to get tentative or shut down. Somehow our fragile male egos operate under the impression that we have to get it all right all of the time. Don't get caught in that trap, and don't collapse when you get it wrong. Simply sense and adjust. Over and over.

She won't make this easy on you because sometimes she'll react strongly when something you try doesn't feel good, particularly if you're not noticing her initial discomfort. Just be aware that most women experience a lot of clumsy lovemaking in their life. Most men simply don't have the skills. So be compassionate for any anger that may have built up over her lifetime at the lack of care and skill of her past lovers, or even you. When you handle her unskillfully, even in a small way, it can trigger that chronic frustration.

If she lashes out, don't retreat, don't collapse, don't pull back. Just stay with her and adjust. Your responsiveness will settle her quickly. Assure her that you are committed to being attuned to her body. The more you do it, the more she'll feel that attunement, the more she'll trust you, and the gentler her reactions will become over time.

WARMING HER UP

By putting these conditions in place, you're creating the container in which your woman can start to open sexually. Now, it is time to warm her up.

You already know that women warm up more slowly than men. And, like most men, you probably find it frustrating. You wish your woman would grab your crotch right away and just get to the action. But she's different. She probably doesn't go for your genitals right out of the gate, and she absolutely does NOT want you to grab her yoni right away. She's craving that you have the skill to slowly bring her into a state of arousal.

In fact, this is **the number one complaint of women in the sexual arena: men go too fast.** If you're going to lead her skillfully in sex, slow down. Take your time. And warm her up. I'm reminded of a poem titled "If You Want Me", by Ellen Bass:

you must approach
quietly as a doe
to the river for her evening drink
you must be slow as the
ripening of wood
with the patience of a village of weavers
bringing into the one perfect carpet

This poem speaks perfectly to the Feminine's inherent vulnerability, which is magnified and exposed in the domain of sex. The Feminine can't be rushed into sex. You must lead her into openness.

This chapter will walk you through a number of techniques for doing so. They are presented in order of increasing intensity. It is a sensible progression, but certainly not a defined sequence that you follow. Consider them tools in your toolkit.

The first technique is **Foreplay Throughout the Day**. For women, foreplay does not begin when you get into the bedroom. It begins hours and days earlier. If you play it skillfully, you can have her rather warmed up by the time you pass through the bedroom door.

What you must realize is that, unlike men, who think about sex every seven seconds, women usually *aren't* thinking about it. Literally, as they go through a normal day, the topic of sex is like a black hole in their mind. It is up to you to keep it in your woman's consciousness.

You can do this by kissing her deeply first thing in the morning. Wrapping her in a hug and whispering in her ear how badly you wish you could take her back to bed before you leave for work. Texting her during the day how much you miss her lips.

Don't be graphic. Be romantic and sensual, tiptoeing on the edge of sexual. Remember that she's not warmed up yet, so anything too pointed will be a turnoff. Be verbally seductive and she might even surprise you by escalating it herself.

All you are doing is keeping the sensuality at the forefront of her thoughts.

• • •

The second technique is **Slow Body Movements**. Until properly warmed up, the Feminine physiology does not like sudden or jarring movements. So, as it relates to how quickly you physically move your body during sexuality: **move three times slower than you naturally would**. For me, this means I move slowly and deliberately when I:

- Approach her and enter her personal space. I usually reach my arms out to make very light contact with my fingers on her body as a signal that I'm there, and only then do I slowly move my body in close to hers.
- Massage her body. You will be amazed at how hot your woman finds long, VERY slow strokes across her skin with a flat, open hand.
- Pick her up or roll her to a different position on the bed. Slow speed helps you avoid inadvertently twisting one of her limbs the wrong way.
- Navigating your own body and limb movements in proximity to her body. It helps avoid inadvertent bonks which might hurt her and kill the mood.

I was taught a phrase that perfectly characterized things: **You need to move her with control, not force or speed**. So, if you're going to push her onto the bed or up against the wall, you do so not with an abrupt thrust of the hands but rather a slow steady pressure that maintains contact with her until she comes to rest (i.e. on the bed or against the wall).

This doesn't mean that you *always* move slowly. Once she's warmed up, you can mix in certain controlled rapid movements in order to surprise her. But until then, I cannot emphasize this enough: **move three times slower than you naturally would**.

• • •

The next technique is **Kissing**. Most women will tell you that their number one turn on is good kissing. And most American men don't know how to kiss because they were never taught. You probably picked it up on your own as you grew up, and most likely have never gotten honest feedback on it from a woman.

Start by moving into her personal space slowly as discussed before, and give her a few moments to acclimate to the closeness. Maintain eye contact and your breathing while allowing her time to settle.

Move to initiate the kiss and keep your lips soft and slightly open. Women will tell you that a lot of men tighten their lips into a hardened pucker, which doesn't feel good. Keep them relaxed in a soft pucker, extended forward out from the face. Allow your lips to gently press together with hers. Do not use tongue at this stage. Just savor how it feels to be in contact with her.

When you decide to bring the tongue into play, go slowly. Do not push it into her mouth. Simply extend it a half centimeter gently out between your lips as an invitation to her tongue. Wait for her to offer hers.

When she does, maintain the soft pucker and just let the tips of the tongues get to know each other. Then at the right time, proceed further as appropriate.

You can make or break the mood solely on the quality of your kissing. I urge you to master this foundational sexual/sensual skill.

• • •

The fourth technique is **Eye Gazing**. This is a very powerful Tantric technique for establishing a sensual connection between two people. Lead her in this and I guarantee it will open her up.

Sit across from each other with your faces about two to three feet apart, but no closer. Sitting cross-legged can be difficult for many men because tight hamstrings cause you to hunch over, so use stools or pillows.

Simply hold each others' gaze for two minutes, looking into her left eye (don't shift between the two). Blinking is fine, but looking away is not. It is not a staring contest, nor do you need to be intense about it. You simply need to feel into your heart and your love for her. That's it. Just feel. No thoughts. Just be very present with one another.

This practice is powerful. Those not accustomed to it can find it intense, and you may experience nervous laughter. Stick with it and learn to settle into the depth that it can bring to you.

• • •

The next technique is **Breath**. A core Tantric technique is to breathe in sync with your partner. There are many different specific techniques, but I will suggest the most basic. While sitting across from her doing eye gazing or in an embrace while lying on the bed, whisper to her *"Breathe with me. Just follow my breath."* You will then lead her in ten slow, deep breaths. Use the Ujjayi breath we discussed earlier. This allows you to keep the breath on a slow pace, and the audible nature of the Ujjayi helps her hear and follow you.

If you are laying together, you can exaggerate the expansion of your belly with the breath to add an additional physical cue so she can follow your pace.

This is not about trying to create some magical Tantric experience. It serves only to synchronize the two of you in a very visceral way. Remember that for the Feminine, sexuality is an activity of temporary union. Breath and eye gazing are powerful tools for creating this sense of oneness.

• • •

The sixth technique is **Sensual Touch**. Instead of going straight to overt sexuality, you might invite her to receive pleasure from you: "*Baby, lay down on the bed, I'm going to rub your back*" (or feet). You're not rushing things, but rather providing her a pressure-free way to go into her pleasure. Do this without being goal oriented, as she will feel it if you are and it will shut her down. You aren't massaging her in order to GET something, but rather as an act of generosity to her. Pleasure is your gift to her.

Remember to stroke her very, very slowly, as stated before.

And, learn to find your own pleasure in touching her by tuning into the sensations you experience. Also, learn to derive pleasure from seeing her pleasure. It will create a circuit of energy between the two of you that is a virtuous cycle.

• • •

Another technique is Hair Pulling. This is a very powerful way to introduce intense but pleasurable sensation. It is easiest to perform when you're in a chair and she's sitting on the ground in front of you, leaning against you between your legs. This gives you easy access to her head. But you can do it from any position.

Run your fingers through her hair with your palm gliding along her scalp. Your fingers will be separated and the hair will be flowing between them. At some point in mid-stroke, close the gaps between your fingers (they end up all parallel) so they grab the hair between them at the root. Then slowly pull your hand away from her head. The tension between your fingers will create a gentle pull on a whole section of her hair. For most women, this is very pleasurable. The scalp is a place that doesn't get a lot of touch.

After some time warming her up with this, you can take the intensity up a notch. Instead of clamping straight fingers together while stroking her hair, you'll actually (in mid-stroke) gently grab a fistful of hair near the scalp. Slowly tighten the fist to increase the tension on the hair, and hold it. The feeling is intense, so go slowly and allow her to acclimate to the sensation. Also, remember to adjust your hand so all the strands of hair in your grasp have uniform tension on them — it's easy for a small clump to get pulled too much and that will feel painful to her.

You can use advanced hair pulling techniques to play with a little dominance. But for now, use what I've taught you to give your woman sensation and pleasure in pursuit of leading her into a more sexual state.

• • •

The eighth technique is **Sensation Play**. This is a collection of practices which range from mild to wild. All are **designed specifically to wake up her body**. The more you activate her body, the more she gets out of her head and relaxes, a dynamic similar to what we discussed in Chapter 10 on Embodiment. This is the entire point of sensation play. Below I share two specific types for you to initiate with your woman.

First, I recommend bringing sensation to her skin using certain implements. Have her lay down on her belly and give her a back massage. Then consider one of the following:

- Run an ice cube down her back, across her buttocks, and finally to her inner thigh. Expect her to vocalize and wiggle around when you do this.
- Get a soft feather or very soft fur mitt and gently run it across her body.
- Get a soft rope and drag it across various naked parts of her body.

The second technique I recommend is called "drumming", aptly named because you'll be using your hands to do that on various parts of her body. Begin with her laying on her belly on the bed. I start with two fists, thumbs on the top side, and drum very gently on the soft parts of her upper back, then down the sides of her spine. Then I might move to the sacrum, a spot that holds a lot of energy in the body.

I'll then proceed with open hands to drum on her buttocks. You can vary the angle and speed across all parts of the buttocks, and include the thighs as well. Finally, if I can feel her getting warmed up, I'll spread her legs apart a little bit and start to slowly drum on the lower buttocks and inner thighs closer to her yoni. The impact of the drumming reverberates up into the yoni and can be a turn on for many women. It is an easy way to stimulate her without even touching her genitals.

Note that drumming is just a mild form of Impact Play, which is a larger category of activities that includes spanking. I will give just a short introduction here.

Consensual spanking is a great activity for creating exciting sexual play with your woman. Unfortunately, it has a negative stigma attached to it. Many picture it in their minds as sadistic punishment of an unwilling recipient. But I'm talking about spanking between consenting adults for the purposes of play. The physicality of it serves to wake the body up (just like the drumming, but a little more intensely) and creates a playful power dynamic which can increase the sexual Polarity between you two.

Spanking can happen in many positions. An occasional spank while you enter your woman from behind. Putting her over your knee for a playful ritual spanking. Having her stand and lean forward with her hands on a table. I encourage you to direct her into these positions. Pay attention, though, to what feels consensual and fun for her.

You can spank her just a few times — as an ingredient you sprinkle in. Or you could set up a slow rhythmic spanking that goes on for a minute or more. It can create a hypnotic effect.

You can create a semi-humorous context. Like giving her a "bad girl" spanking for being late to meet you. Or a "good girl" spanking for planning such a nice birthday celebration for you. This good girl/bad girl theme is a juicy one.

Whatever the form, I'll offer these short suggestions. One, proceed slowly and closely track her state. Only continue if she's consenting and enjoying the pleasure/sensation combo. Two, immediately follow any hard smack with a few seconds of gentle caressing of the area of impact, which balances the intense sensation. Three, use a slightly cupped hand rather than a flat hand. This will create more "thud" than "smack". Finally, always spank from the bottom up on the buttock rather than the top down. It will feel better to her.

Done well, spanking is one vehicle for leading your woman to her sexual edge. Move into it slowly, starting with the drumming and progressing over the course of many sessions with your woman.

• • •

The next technique is **Restraint**. This category includes any activity that constricts the movement of her body. You do this because the act of restraining her body in some way forces her to surrender into the control of the constraint. She has the choice in the moment to either fruitlessly struggle, or to give in. For a woman who goes about her day in full control of her choices and her body, restraint can playfully but powerfully bring her into a more surrendered state. It's an effect similar to that of swaddling babies — it takes away choice, induces surrender, and makes them feel safe.

If you've set up a safe container, her surrendered state should expand into feelings of relaxation and trust. And for a Feminine adult, this surrendered state can be a gateway to sexual arousal.

And, yes, this is why people do rope bondage, which also has a negative stigma of something akin to a kidnapping: someone is grabbed and forcibly tied up against their will. It is not like that. Like spanking, it is a consensual activity that can be done with a lot of presence, love, and mutual participation. And certain Japanese forms of rope bondage are characterized by a physical beauty of the knots and ropes which appeals to the Feminine side of many women.

But before we talk about ropes (which are an advanced topic), I will present to you some of the restraint techniques which I use and my woman loves. These use only the body. And if you'll tolerate a little hyperbole: these are gold. Very easy ways to create a feeling of safety in your woman.

The first one I call the Straitjacket Hug because the recipient's arms are constrained. It is simple. In a standing position, I pull my woman's arms into her chest, elbows pointed down and hands in loose fists with palms touching her body just below her chin. I stand in front of her and wrap my arms around her upper arms and torso in a hug. My arms and chest press her arms against her body. Instead of a traditional hug, which is symmetrical and mutual, this is me wrapping her up and constraining her. Hold for fifteen seconds and breathe together. Be careful not to put any downward pressure on her body.

The second is the Mummy Hug. With her laying on her back and me on top of her, my legs are parallel to and on the outside of hers. I pull my legs toward each other, pressing inward at both the knees and the ankles. This effectively immobilizes her legs. I then prop myself up on my elbows, but pull my elbows toward each other in order to pin her own arms to the sides of her torso. I then cross her hands in front of her chest and the weight of my chest holds them down. My hands and forearms can just be beside her, or I can put them under her shoulder blades. Hold for a little while. My woman experiences a big sense of relaxation from this whole-body wrap. Note that you can actually have intercourse in this position as well.

My woman pointed out an interesting effect of having her legs pinned together like this. She said that men spend so much energy trying to get their woman's legs apart, that holding her legs together can have the opposite effect: it can increase arousal and actually have her want to open her legs *more* to her man. Reverse psychology at its finest.

The last one is my favorite. My woman loves it. I call it the Butt Hug. With her lying on her back on the bed, I position myself between her legs with my chest at her yoni. I wrap my arms around her hips, and my hands either grasp her buttocks or sit flat with palms against the small of her back. I squeeze her hips with firm pressure from all sides.

There are multiple elements happening here:

- The pressure from my arms around her hips is grounding for her.
- Although her legs are open, I'm firmly covering her yoni with my chest, which makes her feel safe.
- The rising and falling of my breath against her yoni is stimulating.

If your woman responds like mine, she'll experience a deep settling and sense of healing safety in her body from this Butt Hug.

Let me finish with a few words about rope bondage. It has a negative stigma for most. But I feel it is a big missed opportunity for couples. It can be a mutually pleasurable, erotic, and satisfying experience for both partners.

You set up a suitable space on the floor with mats. Light candles and turn on some appropriate mood music. Ask her to lay down and you'll begin to apply the ropes in a tie that you learned from any of the plentiful resources available. Maybe a chest harness (which you can use to move her body around, and also provides nice pressure on her torso) or one that holds her arms behind her back (giving you free access to tease and tantalize her front side using different types of Sensation Play).

During the entire application process, you two are connected through eye contact and verbal communication. You're checking in with her if a specific knot or tie is comfortable. She's expressing to you feelings of relaxation.

The combination of this restraint and sensation play is powerful — she has no choice but to surrender into the sensation and your control. This is an amazing way for consenting adults to create a lot of sexual intensity and fun. You will be the man who takes her to her sexual edge.

• • •

The next technique is **Dirty Talk**. Talking dirty with your woman is one of the most effective ways to turn up the Polarity and intensity of your sexuality. Yet few men do it well, if at all. I didn't in my marriage. It was a skill I learned later.

Trust me — it *is* a learnable skill and you *can* do it. And it's rather fun if you can get past your initial resistance. Shame might hold you back and create anxiety. You may know the words you *want* to say, but will be unable to vocalize them. Don't worry — practice and learning some basic material will get you through this.

Let's jump right in. You'll need to get over any reluctance around uttering "naughty" words. Simple litmus test: if you can't comfortably say the words "cock" or "pussy" in your sexy talk with your woman, then you probably have a basic mental block. These are words you were told your whole life not to use. And it is this taboo that makes them so hot to now use with your woman.

It might help to look at some examples of dirty talk. I divide this into three categories: mild, medium, and spicy, and will share examples below.

In the mild category, you aren't using much explicit language. Rather the goal is to be positive, complimentary, and sexually suggestive. In fact, I would not even call it "dirty". But it is edgier talk than most men use.

Some examples are:

- *"I love when you touch me like that."* If your partner is doing something that feels good, tell them so. They'll be encouraged by it and are much more likely to do it again in the future.
- *"Your ass looks amazing in that dress."* You might say this while the two of you are out to dinner. It reminds her that she is a sexual being, and can create arousal even before getting to the bedroom.
- *"It feels so good to be inside you."* Whisper this in her ear after you penetrate her. You are commenting on something happening directly in the present moment, which should help make her more present.

In the medium category, you are going to get more explicit about describing sexual acts or intentions. Mild dominance is introduced as a theme. But it leaves out some of the more hardcore phrases. This level of talk is appropriate after things have become sexual and she's turned on:

- *"I'm going to make your pussy purr."* It is both playful and directly sexual. It lets her know that you'll be taking the lead to pleasure her.
- *"You are such a naughty/dirty little vixen."* Being called naughty is slightly edgy. You're playfully accusing her of being a bad girl.
- *"Get down on your hands and knees."* Explicit commands done well can be extremely stimulating to the Feminine. They are the

ultimate manifestation of you setting direction into which she can surrender.

- *"Now, are you going to be a good girl and do everything I tell you tonight? Or a bad girl that needs to be spanked?"* You're verbally establishing dominance. This sets up two scenarios, both of which provide for a playful power imbalance.

Finally, we have the spicy category of talk. It's edgy, explicit, and sometimes bordering on taboo. It can be dominant to the point of being slightly humiliating. So it is important that you only use this in a high-trust relationship, and only when she's really turned on. You'll be amazed at how the same words can be either arousing or repugnant to the Feminine depending on how turned on she is.

I've chosen not to include examples of spicy talk in this work. Check my website for future resources covering this topic.

Now, knowing the words is only half the battle. Your delivery is just as important. If you can't confidently deliver them, you'll just look silly. The key is to say them with a steady voice, strong eye contact, and not a hint of wavering. You have to "hold the pose".

Practice makes perfect, and that is what you're going to do when you're alone at home. Stand in front of a mirror, look yourself in the eye (although visualize her eyes), and practice saying some of the phrases.

The pitch of your voice is important here. Let it settle down into its lowest natural tenor. Practice this. Speak slowly, enunciate, and be loud enough that she's sure to hear you. Having to repeat yourself dampens the effect.

As you grow more comfortable, try to connect the words to your own desire and power. Repeat over and over until you feel them coming from your gut, not just your head. Repeat until you can eradicate any tentativeness or attachment to her response. Practice until you know your woman will hear and feel your conviction and command.

Remember that less is more. Be succinct, and just let it land in her.

• • •

The final technique is **Yoni Stimulation**. Most men go straight here after just a few minutes of kissing and fondling. But notice how many warm-up techniques we've discussed that you can use that don't involve the yoni itself. I encourage you to take your time in getting here.

The yoni is a uniquely sensitive part of a woman. For some women, it stores years of any sexual shame or trauma they may have experienced. There is a vulnerability about it that you can't understand.

And it is not naturally ready to go like your genitals are. Even a long-time wife or girlfriend does not want you to stimulate her yoni without some suitable warm up.

You'll want to start by bringing blood flow into the area without directly touching the yoni yet. Rub and squeeze the inner thighs and buttocks. Get her used to sensation in this area.

When you do make contact with the yoni, make it slow. I sometimes like to just cup my hand against it, pressing my palm down on the pubic bone with fingers flat against and covering the vaginal opening. The pressure and stillness have the effect of introducing direct touch while still maintaining the feeling of safety. When she acclimates to the direct touch, you can begin to slowly move your hand in tiny circles to add some movement.

At this point, she may be ready for more direct stimulation. It will help if you have some knowledge of female anatomy. One important thing to know is that the clitoris is not just at the top of the vaginal opening under the hood, but also extends down inside the lips. So instead of going straight for the clitoris and hood, you can gently squeeze and pull on the lips to create arousal and more blood engorgement in the area. The more engorgement, the more receptive she is to your touch here.

You may choose to orally stimulate her. Most women will love it when you do. In fact, many women lament their male partner's lack of willingness and/or skill in this area. Let me give you just a few basic tips in this arena:

- Many women have shame around their vagina. One of the most relaxing things a man can do for his woman is "yoni worship" — overtly savoring the sight, smell, and taste. Personally, I've come to find the musky smell of my woman's yoni to be incredibly intoxicating. It is an earthy, primal scent, an experience akin to what musky colognes try to emulate. You will be amazed at the effect a little expressed appreciation can have on her.
- Learn to apply a soft, flat tongue at all times rather than an extended, pointy, and hard tongue. It makes a huge difference that she can feel.
- Start with very slow tongue movement on the lips first, then follow by finally making slow contact with the clitoris itself (through the hood). Just give little light touches to the clit at first before moving to longer strokes.

- Make more of the movement with the tongue rather than the head. It will feel more calming to her if you keep your head still.

There is much more around oral sex that we could go into here, but I've laid out enough for you to understand how to get started.

CONCLUSION

If your woman isn't as open to sex as she used to be, don't blame her. Use what I've shared to evaluate how well you've created the right container for sexuality, and how well you've developed the skills and courage to slowly lead her into pleasure. It is not just about going straight to intercourse — it's much more sophisticated than that. Have the skill and the patience to set direction and provide structure in the bedroom in a way that no man has before for her.

ELEMENT 3

CREATE **SAFETY**

In this section, we explore the third element of our Blueprint for a Masculine core: creating safety for your woman. The Feminine retracts when it doesn't feel safe, and flourishes when it does.

In Chapter 14, we'll explore the challenges of navigating your woman's intense emotions. Ironically, they can provide an opportunity to strengthen trust. The more you master these skills, the safer she will feel emotionally.

In Chapter 15, we'll explore something that has a huge effect on her emotional safety but is not natural for most men: being in your heart.

Your ability to create financial safety for her (as a Provider), as well as physical safety (as a Protector), are also both critical. However, due to space constraints, I have chosen to defer those topics to a subsequent work.

CHAPTER 14

YOUR WOMAN

Your Masculine leadership is MOST needed when your woman is upset. Yet, it is also, by FAR, the most difficult time to manifest it.

The Feminine is moody. You might even say that the Feminine is "crazy", particularly when she is ranting and raving at you. It feels like she is blaming you. Mixing together disparate topics, facts, and distortions. Shaming you. Giving you the cold shoulder. Distrusting you. Closing her body to you.

In those times, she may seem scary and impenetrable. It may seem like the primal connection between the two of you is impaired. You feel like either fighting back or giving up. And you're utterly confused because her reactions don't seem to make sense based on the circumstances. Her emotions seem to rise up out of nowhere, in a fury.

I have good news for you — it actually all makes perfect sense. But you're going to have to radically shift your perspective in order to understand why.

SHE IS VULNERABLE INSIDE

Before I give you the secret, there is one thing you need to understand: **inside of every woman, even the powerful ones, lies an intensely vulnerable inner core.** Underneath the wisdom, smarts, competence, energy, and power lies an inner child, a little girl that just wants her Daddy to protect her and take care of things. She wants to be seen and loved.

Part of her vulnerability lies in the fact that her Feminine nature is wired to experience emotion far more intensely than a man would. In her relationships, she's going to feel anger, sadness, fear, and disappointment (alongside joy and love) more acutely than you would. So, circumstances that make you feel a twinge of sadness or anger may cause a tsunami of intense feelings in her. The volume knob is simply turned up louder.

And if she's had trauma in her background, or is in a state of threat in the moment, her reactions will be even more amplified. She does not have your capacity to suppress emotion, so for most women the highs are higher and the lows are lower.

Many women also feel physically vulnerable around men, who are in most cases bigger and stronger. We may live in a civilized society, but women must rely on that civility for their safety. Many will tell you that they often feel some level of risk, no matter how remote, and must deal with that on a daily basis. In fact, many women have actually been the victims of some form of sexual assault and carry the emotional wounding that it creates.

So, women tend to have much stronger reactions to situations that make them feel physically and/or emotionally unsafe. In that state, your woman may regress to a less emotionally healthy state and either close down to you or lash out at you.

But when she feels safe, she's more likely to relax and open.

Here are some common examples of things that make the Feminine feel emotionally unsafe:

- *Having her emotions, opinions, or experience denied, ignored, or invalidated by you.* Imagine that she says to you that she's upset that you're going on a golf weekend with your buddies, and your response is "*That's ridiculous. I told you about this two months ago and you agreed.*" Yes, she did agree, but at a gut level she still feels upset. If you tell her it's ridiculous to feel that way (even though she actually does), you're denying her actual experience. This makes her feel unseen for who she really is in this moment. She also feels let down, because she's expecting you to be her rock when she's experiencing a lot of emotion, yet you're telling her in so many words that she somehow needs to be feeling something different than she actually is. The goal is not to figure out who's right, but rather to acknowledge reality in the moment, no matter how crazy it seems.

- *Being left to handle something at which she's not competent.* She looks to her man to help her with hard things in life (just as she helps you with things that are hard for you). When you don't, she feels abandoned. I can remember a time years ago when my woman (with whom I had not yet joined my life or finances) got very upset with me after I didn't offer to help her with her taxes one year. I had all of my excuses why I'd been extremely busy in that time frame with my own life responsibilities. Nonetheless, she was left to fend for herself on a task which she found particularly challenging. She did not feel taken care of by me.

- *You forgetting something that is important to her,* such as bringing home the milk, fixing the jammed window, or remembering an anniversary. You might think these are little things, but she experiences these lapses as evidence that she is not important to you, and that she cannot trust you to follow through. This will happen anytime you don't do what you said you would do. Imagine a situation in which you've promised for weeks that you'd get the car's oil changed. She blows up when she asks about it and you say that you still haven't gotten it done. You're completely surprised by the intensity of her reaction. To you, it is not a big deal. To her, it is a sign that you're not paying enough attention and taking care of things.

- *Feeling your fear, indecisiveness, or lack of direction.* When she doesn't feel your Masculine gift of clarity and direction, she trusts you less and naturally must go into her own Masculine in order to take care of things. She feels less safe when you don't have things handled.

- *Not feeling you present.* When you aren't in the moment, it feels to her as if she is not important to you. She experiences this as a lack of love and a break in the connection between the two of you. When she lashes out at you for looking at your phone during your dinner date, it is because she doesn't feel you there with her. This is very upsetting to her psyche. Your protestations that *"I was just making sure nothing important was happening at work. We have a big project going!"* mean nothing to her. Yes, she knows she's being sensitive. But she needs to feel your attention is with her.

- *You hiding or denying your emotions.* She's a sensitive Feminine be-ing. When you don't own and share your emotions, she can't feel the connection between the two of you. It can be very disturbing to the Feminine psyche when she feels something and you're not acknowledging it. It is crazymaking and makes her feel unsafe.

Most experiences that create a sense of emotional unsafety for her tend to fall into two categories: either you failed to love her, or you failed to lead her. It's a gross simplification, but fits well enough and helps sim-plify the approach to a remedy. Because you CAN consciously affect the situation.

Things that make her feel loved can include:

- *Verbal expressions of love.* This is the most common way — the simple "*I love you.*" But remember that communication is 70 percent non-verbal. So the inclusion of eye contact, breath, and speaking from the heart make all the difference in how deeply this phrase is received. In my relationship, I do the occasional throw-away verbal "*I love you*", but sometimes I pull my woman close, look her in the eye, breathe with her for a second, and wait for the feeling of love to actually well up within me before I ver-balize it. This has a big impact on her.
- *Doing things for her.* For most women, verbal expressions are not enough. Sometimes the things you *do* for her loom larger. Things with which she struggles offer the best chance to make her feel loved. You feed this part of her when you notice ways in which you can help her, and don't wait for her to ask for help. I recently sat with my woman and helped her plow through the red tape to get her business license renewal completed. I was proactive in

offering and helping her with this, and she felt very loved and taken care of.

- *Opening your heart to her.* This means sharing your inner self from a heartful place rather than an intellectual one. When I am vulnerable with my woman and make space for her feelings, she feels a love connection with me that powerfully opens her. We will talk more about this in Chapter 15.

- *Tracking what's important to her.* When your woman feels that she is in your field of attention, she feels loved. Years ago when I was checking in with my woman periodically about how well she was dealing with the fact that an uncle was battling serious cancer, she felt remembered. Do you know what is emotionally or logistically alive for your woman in her life at the moment? She needs to feel that she's a priority among all of your otherworldly endeavors. She does NOT want to feel forgotten, because to her Feminine heart this indicates a lack of love and care. Sadly, most women will tell you that they're tracking more in their man's life than their man is tracking in theirs.

Things you do that have her feel led include (these are more brief since this entire book is about this kind of leadership):

- Setting direction for the two of you so that she can feel some temporary relief from the burdens of decision making
- Providing structure and setting boundaries within which she can relax and flow
- Knowing what you want and being decisive
- Staying grounded in the face of her emotional storms
- Tuning into her needs, anticipating them, and taking action on them

IT'S NOT CRAZY

When you provide these things, the Feminine relaxes. She feels loved and led. Which then brings us to the secret I said I would share with you about your woman's emotional chaos. Her behavior is explained by one simple maxim which I've derived from something I learned from David Deida: **90 percent of the "crazy" comes from your woman not feeling loved and led.** So the next time your woman gets irrationally emotional or mad at you, know that the root of it is that she is probably not feeling a strong connection between the two of you, not feeling your care for her, or not feeling your leadership, groundedness, and direction.

Her emotional reactions are going to seem over the top or misplaced to you. But they are your signal that she's in pain because she's not feeling loved and led by you.

That's a very different lens through which to see it than "*She's being a bitch*" or "*She acting crazy.*" Next time you find yourself thinking these things, just try to reframe her behavior as that of someone who is not feeling loved or led by you. She's suffering because of it.

Consider it a gift rather than a burden. She's showing you through her emotional reactions where you're not showing up in your full Masculine. Follow the breadcrumbs back to find the ways in which you're not loving or leading her. I posit that more often than not you'll find the cause rooted in your own behavior.

David Deida says that the complaint she's presenting is often not really about the content of the complaint. And I add that the magnitude of her reaction is not always proportional to the issue at hand. Rather,

both indicate a lack of safety or connection created by a lack of your love and leadership.

Her emotional meltdowns may make NO sense given the overt circumstances. But they DO make sense in the context of the underlying emotion.

In my example about my woman's taxes, it doesn't make sense for her to be upset in the context of me genuinely and honestly being too busy to help her at that time. We never had an agreement I would, and it was not even necessarily an area in which I excelled. But at the primal level, it makes sense that she would feel frantic about the taxes because it is not her strength. And if she's in that state, it makes much more sense that she might unfairly blame me and unintentionally lash out.

Her flare-ups arise unexpectedly. Labeling them as "crazy" would just be my unskillful way of dealing with my confusion over this unexpected reaction. But that label doesn't lead to greater understanding or closeness. It just creates more separation.

So if you want to lead your relationship from your Masculine core, don't separate yourself. Don't chase your tail trying to fix the complaint itself. And don't wait for her to solve her own emotional problems or calm herself down. Rather, figure out where you're not demonstrating your love (in ways that SHE feels) and where you're not leading her. After that is addressed, you can look at the content of the complaint.

Stop blaming her. **Your upset and scary woman is actually hurting**. She's in a state of threat underneath and feeling her vulnerable, scared part. See her through this lens and take matters into your own hands. **Lead** her out of this state.

In my own relationship, it actually took me several years to really see this part of my woman. She moves so powerfully and capably through the world that I didn't recognize her vulnerable side. Once I did, it softened how I perceived her emotions and moods. I was able to more proactively lead her out of her chaos. And more importantly, she started to feel really seen and taken care of by me. As a result, we started having fewer fights and more sex.

Don't be like the 95 percent of men who can't see their woman's intensely vulnerable side. It exists right alongside her strong side, and the two are not mutually exclusive.

THE WRONG WAY TO REACT

As counterintuitive as it may seem, the times that a woman is most challenging to you is usually when she's feeling the most unsafe. And it's when she is most longing for a strong man who can "handle her". Who can be with her emotional chaos and vulnerability, not run from it. Who can love and lead her in a way that settles her Feminine nervous system. Who will finally recognize her vulnerable side and take care of it. Can you be that man for her?

Unfortunately, 95 percent of men don't rise to the challenge. Most of them make things worse.

One typical reaction is to go into a freeze state when her emotions flare up so quickly and intensely. You don't know what to say or do, so all you are capable of is sitting there silently — numb and dumb. Unfortunately, this type of non-engagement (even if it is not intentional) enrages her. She will not feel loved.

An extension of the freeze state is when you withdraw or shut down. You exit the conversation and/or give her the cold shoulder. The message you're sending, either implicitly or explicitly, is *"I can't talk with you until you calm yourself down."* Or, you might stay in the conversation, but stone-faced and silent. It is a quiet *"Fuck you"*. Both withdrawal and shutdown leave her feeling abandoned to deal with her emotions alone, right when she needs you the most. She will feel neither loved nor led.

Another type of reaction is when you collapse in the face of her emotions. This entails profuse and compulsive apologizing, feeling sorry for yourself, or other Approval Seeking Behavior. Anything to make the intensity stop. I think it goes without saying that your woman won't be feeling led by you when you're in this reactive state. She'll experience you as a supplicating wuss.

And now we arrive at the granddaddy of all reactions to your woman's emotional chaos: defensiveness. When she's hurling chaotic emotions at you or blaming you for something you did, real or not, you're going to want to make it stop at all costs. So you're going to become what my therapist affectionately calls "Fix the Facts Guy." You'll deny what she claims. Try to correct her incorrect perceptions of the facts. Or use blame to convince her that her own actions are the cause.

The compulsion to get defensive is so strong because, in her emotional state, she's probably not being entirely logical. She may be exaggerating, twisting the truth, using faulty logic, tying together multiple separate issues, or bringing up hurts from years ago. Your logical Masculine nature will be in utter disbelief that she could get this worked up using that illogical logic.

You'll then say to yourself "*Oh, she's upset because she misunderstands a few things. If I can clear them up for her, she'll stop being upset.*" Good luck with that, my friend. The truth is that rarely can new information stop a woman's emotional chaos in the moment. But that is what defensiveness usually looks like: responding to emotion with an intellectual response.

It's like trying to stop an ocean wave. It doesn't work. The emotional tsunami can't be stopped like that. So, better to turn and ride the wave of emotion for the moment. Worry about the information later, once the wave loses steam.

You have to remember this: don't take her emotional attack literally. Don't try to defend yourself from the words that come out of her mouth using words coming out of your mouth. First, see this for what it is: an expression of her pain.

If you want to be successful in this interaction with her, you need to meet her emotion with your empathy and open heart. Not with intellect and information. Never try to "fix the facts" when she's emotional. It will only enrage her and make her believe you are an emotional black hole. That you can't be trusted to create safety for her emotions and her heart.

Let's look again at the example in which she's upset that you're going on a golf weekend with your friends. For you to say "*That's ridiculous. I told you about this two months ago and you agreed!*" is just you trying to correct the facts in her mind. It is a fully intellectual response. Seems completely logical. And, it will fail. Miserably. Because it doesn't in any way tune into the fact that she's hurting. She knows damn well that she previously agreed to it. But she's hurting nonetheless. In this example, I'd guess that she's feeling a lack of connection between the two of you, and may be harboring a story that she's not a priority for you. Your impending absence plays into that story. It is actually irrelevant whether that story is ridiculous. What's important is that you tune into whatever pain she's feeling rather than try to fix the facts.

To successfully engage with an emotional woman, you must respond at the emotional level (which we'll discuss shortly). Defending and explaining just makes things worse.

So, why do you keep doing it? Because of your Masculine wiring. **The Masculine just wants to "do it right".** To succeed in life's tasks. For things to be logical and linear. And, above all, for your woman to trust you. An unhappy or angry partner can feel like living proof that you are, in fact, failing at all of that. It's usually not true. But it feels like that.

And if you have abandonment issues, it gets worse because your subconscious believes that a partner that is angry with you will leave you. Her intense negative emotions strike right at the core of your psyche, and you'll want to make them stop **at all costs**.

But you're not crazy. In many cases, her attacks are, in fact, unfair and based on faulty logic. So what is a man to do?

FIRST, HEAR HER PAIN

The question becomes: how can you successfully handle your emotional woman? Below I will lay out all that I believe is relevant here.

First, you must **learn to weather the initial storm**. This is nothing more than the capacity to Respond vs. React that we've been discussing. It is your nervous system's capacity to withstand that initial wave of her emotional intensity. To stay present and not react just yet. You will develop this capacity using some of the techniques in this book.

You can also help yourself by not trying to make it stop. Just swim in it. Revel in it. Learn to love the feeling of being misunderstood or blamed. Tell yourself that it means you are important to her, rather than playing a victim and seeing it as abuse or her "crazy". Tell yourself that everything is going to be OK — she's not going to leave you and you have nothing to lose. Anything to reduce the stakes and avoid reacting.

Remember that her emotions are a transient event. They are an organic arising of energy in her that may or may not be supported by reality. That is the true nature of the Feminine. It feels what it feels, and it doesn't need to be all figured out in the moment. And it is likely to change in the next moment. So can you **allow her to just feel what she feels without bringing yourself into the narrative**? Don't make it about you in those first few moments. Even when she's blaming you. Feel her first. You'll have time for your part shortly.

All you are doing in this first stage is holding space for her emotion. Just being there, fully present to receive what she has to share. Without trying to analyze, fix, or change it. Of course, this is easier said than done because she's probably going to be blaming you for the emotions she's feeling. **This is what happens when the Feminine shows its toxic side — feelings are shared along with a lot of blame, anger, and shaming.** You can't help but feel the impact of this and get hooked by it.

Let me reiterate: you WILL get hooked by it.

So I offer you a powerful technique for being with Feminine emotional intensity: **hear the pain, not the blame**. While her words say *"Look what you did..."*, the message underneath is *"I'm hurting."* If you listen to the words, you'll compulsively defend or withdraw. If you listen to the pain underneath, your natural care for her will kick in. You will find it infinitely easier to stay present and engaged with her because you know it is the vulnerable part of her Feminine nature which is hurting.

Remember that Feminine communication is different. It conveys emotion, while Masculine communication is focused on information. She certainly transmits information as well, but it gets amplified by the emotion and level of threat she's experiencing. I encourage you to hear the core message but don't get reactive to the amplification.

Of course, you *should* use the amplification as an important data point: the greater the amplitude of the amplification, the more pain you know she's feeling. But use it only as more information, rather than something to which you need to react.

Make no mistake: this will be extremely hard to do in practice. Because the toxicity is covertly smuggled in with the pain, it is very hard to separate the two.

It can help to imagine her as your young child who is upset. You wouldn't recoil from the child. You'd see her in pain and want to take care of her. **Seeing the little girl in her rather than the powerful raging woman in these moments is an effective way to quell your own reactivity** and stay open to her pain.

But the alternative, your defensiveness, is painful for her. She thinks she's clearly communicating that she's hurting. But all you can hear is her attacking you with suspect information or logic. When you start trying to correct her information or her logic, she feels like you're telling her she shouldn't feel the way she feels. That you're invalidating her experience. That she's crazy to feel this way. This usually only leads to enraging her further.

So don't try to fix or change anything *in the moment* (there's time for that later as appropriate), and don't suggest to her that she fix her emotional problem. Remember that for the Feminine, emotions change by the minute. **Getting hooked on any single one of her emotional expressions is going to cause mutual reactivity that suddenly becomes the problem itself.** All you have to do right now is stay present to the emotion, stay in connection with her, and feel empathy for her pain.

Does this mean you're ignoring the actual content of her complaint? Or that your lack of defensiveness implies that you agree with her logic and conclusions? No, it does not, because you're going to be guided by a powerful corollary principle: **feelings first, facts later**. At first, just hear the pain she's expressing and temporarily ignore her story around it. Don't react to her blame. Ignore the anxiety rising within you and the urge to explain or defend yourself. You will have your chance to respond to the facts later. For now, this is a sequencing exercise.

Trying to reason with someone in an emotional state is like talking French to an English speaker — you're not speaking the same language so you're not going to get through to her. Addressing emotion in the moment with cognitive reasoning almost NEVER works.

When you learn this sequencing technique, you'll find that your defensiveness organically diminishes. Knowing that you will get to the facts later allows you to put them aside momentarily and be present with what's real in the moment: her feelings. Instead of scrambling to explain or defend so you're not in trouble, you are freed up to tune into the fact that your beloved is hurting and she needs your support.

So I encourage you to explicitly invite her to share her pain and her heart with you. Whatever words you end up using, her heart is hoping to hear something to the effect of: *"Wow, you're really upset. OK, I'm here. Tell me how you're hurting."* Focus on an acknowledgment of her state, assurance that you are going to be her rock, and an invitation to share the pain she's feeling. The Feminine is craving this type of response, and craving a man who can provide it. Be that man for her.

The quickest way to the sex, connection, playfulness, and happiness that you're craving is, counterintuitively, straight through her pain.

When you've heard her pain and are ready to respond, you have a number of choices. Below, I will discuss six primary options: empathy, responsibility, curiosity, humor, delay, and boundaries.

RESPOND WITH EMPATHY

By far, the best response you can choose is empathy. Empathy is defined as "the ability to understand and share the feelings of another". Put simply, it is an acknowledgment of another person's feelings, without trying to make those feelings wrong. It doesn't mean you agree with the story around the feelings. Only that you acknowledge that the feelings exist, have some understanding of why THEY feel this way, and allow yourself to feel them yourself.

Your woman's emotions may often seem absurd to you, but the undeniable truth is that she DOES feel this way in the moment. To make her think that she SHOULDN'T feel that way is simply a denial of reality. To make an emotional person feel like they're crazy for feeling the way they do is, in fact, crazymaking.

That is why empathy is so nourishing to your woman. She usually knows when she's being overly emotional and irrational. And she doesn't <u>want</u> to feel that way. She just can't stop it in the moment. It is often the result of years (likely predating but including those with you) of feeling invalidated or unmet in her needs, which builds up and erupts out of her. So your empathy goes a long way toward settling her down. More importantly, it creates a huge sense of safety for her. She knows that no matter how emotionally chaotic she gets, you won't wrong her and you'll seek to understand.

Empathy can take many forms. The most basic form is to simply acknowledge her emotion. Don't try to play therapist — just acknowledge what seems true: "*Wow, this is really upsetting you*" or "*Oh Baby, I'm sorry, I can see I've really upset you.*"

This acknowledgment is a great first step, but you must go further. The next step is to affirm. I like to borrow a phrase from Harville Hendrix's teaching: "*That makes sense.*" Given what you may have said or done (or at how she might have reasonably perceived it), it makes sense that she might feel the way she does.

This could be tough for you. Her interpretation or reaction may, in fact, seem crazy to you. Which will cause you to resist and get defensive. But your ability to open to her reality, no matter how crazy it may seem, is an act of extreme generosity on your part. And that is what empathy requires: generosity to allow that her perspective may have some validity even though it may differ from your reality.

Also, note that real empathy includes being able to FEEL her emotion along with her, not just mentally acknowledging it. For a short time, you join her in the emotion and feel it yourself, rather than just observe it. You may not have experienced her exact circumstances, but you have enough emotional history to draw upon something similar. If she tells you she's feeling forgotten, don't evaluate WHY she feels that way or whether or not she SHOULD feel that way. Rather, you need to simply imagine what it's like to feel forgotten by someone important. I guarantee this will soften you toward her and make you less reactive. This is what real empathy is.

To do this, you have to open your own heart. Unfortunately, so many men live their lives with chronically closed hearts and overly pragmatic minds. With a closed heart and logical mind, you can't feel empathy for her, and thus she can't feel you.

TAKE RESPONSIBILITY

The next way of responding is to take some responsibility for the situation. This option can stand alone, but is more of an adjunct to empathy. First, you feel her pain. Then you take some responsibility for some part of it, even if only a small part. It is highly likely to soften her quickly.

But it is not easy to do.

She may be upset but only partially right about your role in it. Yet your perception is that she's trying to pin the whole thing on you, and you're resisting that.

Or she may be completely misunderstanding some facts or your motivations. You may have had good intentions but simply handled things clumsily (such as phrasing something carelessly).

These things happen for me all of the time in my relationship. When they do, I feel that strong pull to defend and explain myself. Sadly, it almost never works.

What does work is finding some part of the situation to own. For instance, when I am less than skilful in dealing with my woman and she gets upset and escalates the whole situation, I try to circle back and take responsibility for being clumsy and letting things get to this point. I'm not admitting to being bad. I'm admitting to being clumsy. My nervous system seems to find this more palatable, and thus I can circumvent my resistance.

You may think your woman acts crazy at times, but she's probably not 100 percent delusional. There's a kernel of truth in her being upset with you. Find it. Own it.

Once you've done that, you can then take the final step which will really settle her nervous system: tell her what you might do differently in the future so that this doesn't happen again. This is a huge signal to her that you're taking her needs and the health of the relationship seriously. It makes her feel safe that you're course correcting as you go. She will relax.

Now, let's be clear. I'm not saying to take the blame for the whole situation. In most cases there is joint responsibility (usually fifty percent your unconsciousness, fifty percent her overreaction due to her wounding). But a true Masculine leader is not getting caught up in the blame game. He's taking responsibility for leading the couple out of the fighting and toxicity. To do that, he's being proactive in taking responsibility for his part rather than waiting for her to take responsibility for hers.

But absent some clear action to avoid a recurrence of the situation at hand, all you're giving her is vague promises. It won't be enough to fully settle her Feminine nervous system. Empathy is great, but not always enough. Taking responsibility is huge, but not always enough. A true Masculine leader will offer tangible action to ensure it doesn't happen again.

By way of example, my woman was recently upset with me because for over two weeks I hadn't followed up to close out an issue with her accountant that I'd offered to handle. It had been an extremely busy time for me, so I felt a little resentful that she was upset with me. But I owned the fact that I'd let it sit for two weeks. Part of me certainly believed that she needed to back off because she was quite aware that I'd been so busy, and that she should not be so upset with me. But the truth was that I had made a commitment, and breaking it, even for a good reason, impacted her trust in me. So it settled her that I owned that part.

And, I went one step further. I told her that I would start using my task list, which I used extensively at work, to help track things that I promised her. I was disciplined in using it in my work life, so therein lay an opportunity to apply that discipline to my personal responsibilities, including commitments I made to her. My offer of this tangible action to reduce future broken promises was a real trust builder with her.

This trifecta of empathy-responsibility-action gives her the "emotional oxygen" she is desperately needing.

And, once you've done this, THEN you can safely circle back and start to deal with the facts. In other words, you may now correct any inaccurate beliefs from which she was operating, or share how your intentions and motivations were different from what she was assuming.

I wish I had learned these techniques earlier in life. It would have saved me immense heartache and disconnection from my female partners.

I'll share another specific example. Years ago, I had gotten two tickets from my employer to an NBA playoff game that was happening the next night. I was very excited, and my natural instinct was to invite my woman, which I did via text. But during the day it occurred to me that it would be a unique opportunity to really connect with my youngest son, so I changed my mind and decided to invite him instead. I tried throughout the next day to get in touch with my woman via phone so I wouldn't have to disinvite her via text. But I couldn't get through to her because she was so busy that day. Eventually, she sent me a text saying that she needed to know the plan for the game right away so she could plan properly. So, I was forced to disinvite her via text, just hours before the game. She felt hurt and started to close to me. Not because she wouldn't be going to the game, but rather that I wasn't clear about my intentions earlier and therefore she didn't feel taken care of. Of course, I was already feeling bad about disinviting her, so I scrambled to explain my logical reasoning (about the opportunity to connect with my son) and good intentions (around trying to reach her via phone and not wanting to disinvite her via text). And, not surprisingly, this led her to shut down even more to me. I was in a state of anxiety, so I wanted to do anything I could to avoid being the bad guy in this situation. I explained and defended, and in the process left her feeling unheard. It took days for us to repair, and only with the help of our therapist.

I thought I was correcting her misunderstandings. But all she could hear was me implying *"You're crazy to be upset."*

In retrospect, I wish I'd just said from the start *"You're right. I handled this clumsily. It makes sense that you'd feel hurt."* I imagine if I had, it would have taken less than five minutes for her to calm down. And then at that point, I could have circled back and shared that I'd tried to get in touch with her multiple times for the sole purpose of not coldly disinviting her via text. **Because she would have already gotten her emotional oxygen**, she'd have been open enough to appreciate the effort I made and the reasons why I waited to tell her. I would have gotten to the exact place I wanted to get — her understanding what I did and why, and not being mad at me — in much less time. **Ironically, by taking your time, by not going for the frontal assault on facts, you get where you want to be faster**.

Now, this approach does not mean that I didn't think she was being overly sensitive and unfair to me. I do think that, even now. But the whole point here is that if your goal is to get back to a state of play, openness, and connection, it DOES NOT MATTER in the moment that your facts are right or that she's being overly sensitive. Feelings first. Facts later.

Note that this approach need not be a drawn out process, as long as you get the sequencing of feelings before facts right. Recently, someone got upset with me and let me know it via text. Her message ended with *" … and I'm not happy about … .[what you did] … ."* So I texted back *"Oh no. I can see I've caused harm here, so I'm sorry. The truth is that … [explanation of facts], but I see I handled it clumsily and could have been more skillful."* Let's deconstruct this message and how I sequenced it. The first thing I did was to offer empathy and take responsibility

(" ... *I've caused harm* ... "), then I apologized. With that out of the way, I was able to circle back to an explanation of facts and why things innocently came to transpire as they did. I finished by again taking responsibility. It was that simple, all in a short text.

I will also add that when I got this person's initial text, I felt anxiety because I felt embarrassed that I may have done something wrong (even though I had good intentions and pure motives), and a little attacked. But I paused and chose to see her pain being covertly expressed in the message. It immediately softened me and put me in a state of mind to send such a heartful, and ultimately effective, message back.

RESPOND WITH CURIOSITY

There are going to be situations where your woman's emotional response is truly baffling. So when you try to share empathy or tell her "*It makes sense*", you'll actually be faking it and she'll know it. In situations like this, it is better to exercise your curiosity. In other words, first seek to really understand her world before offering any reaction.

In my training in the world of Authentic Relating, I've heard this called "getting shared reality." It is an inquiry into understanding another's reality. It sounds something like: "*Ah, OK. So for you, when I do 'X', it feels like 'Y' to you?*" You are exploring the way she sees things, and constantly syncing with her on each piece of understanding you gain to make sure it is accurate. From this, you'll build a common view of her reality, piece by piece.

So, in the basketball game example shared earlier, instead of being confused by my woman's behavior, I could have gotten curious: "*So, when I texted you to cancel, how did that feel? Oh, you felt unimportant and disregarded? I see. So, because I canceled so late, it felt like you didn't matter to me?"* And so forth. It is just an inquiry. You peel back the layers one by one to really understand where she's coming from.

Then, from this place of shared reality, you can better choose how to react. But you'll find that even just your effort to understand her world will both settle her nervous system and create natural empathy within you.

Nearly all men are baffled by their woman's behavior at times. When you experience this, going the route of curiosity is a wise move.

RESPOND WITH HUMOR

Sometimes, your woman's emotional response will be truly ridiculous. She will be more in the realm of neurosis and her wounds rather than having a valid criticism. Instead of taking her complaint seriously, as you've done so far, you may be better served by going a different route: using humor.

This can take different forms. The "pickup" community has a phrase called "Cocky and Funny", whereby you act cocky and say outrageous stuff to a woman you've just met in order to demonstrate that you are fearless of her reactions. This technique works well in relationship as well, but for the purpose of opening your partner. For instance, my woman was recently genuinely upset at me that I was late in getting to her place because I was watching the World Cup at a bar. She accused me of making the match a higher priority than spending time with her. Of course, I knew the accusation was just a story covering up the pain of her underlying wound of sometimes feeling forgotten. It was her neurosis talking. So, I said *"No, Baby, I wasn't late because of the match. I was late because I was hitting on women at the bar."* She punched me on the arm. And when she punches me on the arm, I know I've diffused the situation. I then grabbed her by the waist, kissed her, and said: "*I'm sorry to make you wait, Love.*"

The reason that this works is that **humor neutralizes drama**. Your woman throws drama at you when she's swimming in her own drama. She's trying to enroll you in her story, and expects that she can hook you into it. Your humor in response is not what she's expecting, so it can shock her out of the drama and remind her of how ridiculous she's being.

Another form of this is using exaggeration. When she throws an accusation or complaint at you, you agree with it and exaggerate. Her: "*You don't even clean up after yourself around here!*" You: "*Yes, Baby, I know. It's terrible. I'm like a caveman. How do you put up with me?! I never take the garbage out, I never run the dishwasher. Yesterday I peed on myself and just decided to fall asleep in the puddle!*"

The humor approach works for one simple reason: it shows you are not intimidated by her emotion or complaint. That you're fearless in the face of her intensity. It demonstrates your Masculine groundedness and is sometimes exactly what she needs. In her state of emotional chaos, she can anchor on the brave certainty you are showing. And if you're funny enough, the humor serves as a battering ram to shake her out of her neurosis.

These techniques are risky. You have to be able to "hold the pose", which means to keep a straight face and not back down when she initially gets angry at your attempt to use humor to demolish her histrionics. If you break character, she'll lose trust in you. The trick is to hold the pose past her point of initial resistance, beyond which the humor opens her.

And, sometimes it doesn't open her up but rather makes her think that you're minimizing what's important to her. So, if the humor is not landing, at some point it is best to pause, drop into your heart, and say something to the effect of "*I'm sorry, Baby. I just wanted to bring a little levity. I'll stop. Tell me how you're hurting.*"

Always remember that humor is just a tool to break the drama cycle, not one for you to avoid dealing with real issues.

ASK FOR A DELAY

Sometimes your woman's emotional state is so intense that it completely blows you out. You don't know whether to fight, cry, or run. Nothing good can come from trying to operate in this state. You'll just end up doing some or all of the things I told you not to do.

In situations like this, I recommend you ask for a temporary pause and delay in the conversation. You say "*Baby, can we pause for a second. I feel myself getting reactive and I really want to hear what you have to say.*" Then do what you need to do, whether it be to take a deep breath, go into the other room for a minute, or take a break for an hour. You just need to assure her that you will promptly re-engage and that her issue is important to you.

This approach is much easier said than done. In the moment, you're caught up in the drama. Knowing that you need to take a break requires you to step outside the drama and see the pattern in which you're caught. My therapist recommended this to me for years before I could successfully do it. You'll need to rely on your "real self" which we discussed in Chapter 7 — the fully-conscious, fully-present, unchanging part of you that is the Watcher. He sits outside the drama and can see when you need a pause.

Mastering this skill will help you immensely. You'll be able to calm down and be more available to hear her pain. It is far more effective than doing a frontal assault on an emotionally charged issue while you're both in a highly elevated state. That's a recipe for a painful fight. Better to take a pause and let the intensity clear.

SET A BOUNDARY

There will be times when your emotional woman's behavior gets so out of bounds that you'll feel you need to set some limits. In other words, you need to set a boundary. I don't go into this topic in depth in this book. But here I will address three common scenarios that can require a boundary.

The first is when she's cutting off connection or giving you the cold shoulder because she's feeling hurt and closed. Personally, I find this type of behavior unacceptable. Yes, there are times when it is best to give my woman space, where she truly needs it to settle and gain perspective. But if I sense that it is punitive in any way, I call it out as something I won't tolerate.

Another scenario is when your woman becomes verbally abusive. My woman generally does not resort to this, but I have been in relationships where my partner did. This is a clear boundary that you should not allow to be crossed. Handle it directly: *"Darling, I'm interested in hearing your pain but have no interest in being insulted. Pause for a second, and let me know if you can come back to your heart. Otherwise, we need to talk later."*

You may encounter scenarios that don't require a boundary per se, but do require some structure. For instance, there have been times where my woman starts to get a little snippy, and I've said: *"No, Baby, we're not fighting right now. I want to connect with you.*" When I use this at the right times, it usually cuts off the friction pretty quickly and leads us back into closeness. Note that you're not telling her to calm down, but rather to be respectful and in her heart.

I also use this technique prophylactically. If we're going on a trip together, I'll sometimes say: "*Ok, Baby, we're going to have fun on this trip together. NO FIGHTING. Just sex and relaxation and exploration. OK, Love?*" The intent is not to shut down her needs or pain. Rather, it is to set a container and an intention to stay in connection.

And remember, sometimes your woman will intentionally try to "poke the bear" (you). If she's feeling forgotten or that you're not being present, she might throw a few jabs at you just to provoke you and elicit a response. To the Feminine, ANY response is better than no response. So when you recognize this behavior in her, instead of setting a boundary you might just ignore the jabs and move on. Or playfully ask her "*Ah, are you trying to poke the bear?*"

SEVEN PRINCIPLES

Now that we've looked at the different options you have for responding to your emotional woman, I'd like to share a collection of principles relevant to this domain.

First, **don't play the victim.** By this I mean to not adopt the frame of "*Ha ha, women are so strange and moody. They are irrational and I can't understand them. You can't ever make them happy. I'll just blame my woman for her outbursts. Or, I'll just do what she tells me and stay out of trouble.*" The fact is that I've explained the dynamic to you. She senses things at an emotional level way more than you do. She feels hurt way more than you do. And so she's going to react far more chaotically than you do. She wants you to love her. She wants you to lead her. When you don't, she gets bitchy and emotional. It's that simple.

You know how she's going to act, and you now know why she acts that way. So instead of playing the hapless victim, accept your role as the person that will lead her out of her occasional dysfunction and back into her heart. Lead the two of you out of conflict and back into connection.

● ● ●

Second, know that **your woman is testing you**. On a continual basis. Most of the time she doesn't know she's doing it. But she notices how you handle her and it gives her information about you. Any guy can talk a big game about being strong and Masculine, about how he will always be there for his woman. But real-world tests cut right through any BS and quickly expose your true nature.

In my experience, I've experienced two primary types of tests. The first test is "*Will he be there for me, even at my worst?*" When you get defensive, withdraw, or attack when your woman gets emotional, she learns that she can't trust you to create a safe space for her to let out her messy emotions. Next time, she'll either amp up the intensity or shut down to you and start turning her attention to other people who can hold space for her.

The second type of test I've experienced is in the vein of "*How much can I control him?*" If you're compulsively going into Approval Seeking Behavior or patiently taking her abuse when she gets mad, then she will know that you don't have boundaries. In this context, she will continue to push you harder to see exactly how much control she can exert over you. She'll take as much as you will give, and keep pushing you until she goads you into setting a boundary. As you prove your lack of backbone, she'll progressively lose respect for you because she knows that she cannot be led by a man with no boundaries. And she knows that if you can't stand up TO her, then you aren't capable of standing up FOR her.

As I said, these tests are usually unconscious on her part. But when they arise, you must make a choice. Are you strong enough to stand your ground, to hold the pose, to skillfully lead her out of her emotional chaos and back to her heart? Or will you run for the nearest exit, back down, or do anything to make the intensity stop?

Now, even when you do hold your ground and "pass a test", don't expect any kind of immediate reward or positive feedback. "Passing" does not always mean that she'll be happy with you. In fact, she may even appear to be angrier if you are holding a boundary or not giving in to her demands. Rarely are you going to get gratification in the moment. It usually comes later as her trust grows and her body and heart open to you. So don't always judge yourself based on her immediate response.

Use these tests as a way to either firmly or playfully display your Masculine solidity, rather than looking at them as a burden. Your woman simply wants to ascertain that you're worthy of leading her. That she can let down her guard and open her heart and her body without fear. This is exactly what you're wanting, and each of these tests she throws your way is an avenue to getting her there. Make the most of these opportunities instead of grumbling about how challenging it is.

• • •

The third principle I will share is to **put the connection before your fear or ego**. In any relationship, it is inevitable that you'll get Feminine intensity thrown at you. This is perfectly natural and nearly universal.

And, of course, your defenses go up when this happens. You protect yourself by defending, explaining, attacking, or withdrawing. Sometimes you find her behavior so exasperating that you want to give up on the conversation, or even the relationship. To just run and hide to get away from her emotion. You pull back, give the cold shoulder, and wait for her to come to you to repair.

Of course, she's feeling the same way, so periods of separation can persist. Unaddressed, these feelings of hurt and separation can turn into layers of sediment that are hard to eradicate.

All of which, of course, contradicts your deeper intention to stand strong and lead your woman. You *want* to hear her pain. You *want* to feel closer to her. You *want* to be a rock for her. You *want* to lead her back to her heart. You *want* to open her up.

Yet despite your intention, you do the exact opposite because you're prioritizing self-protection from fear over the health of the relationship. So, in this context, I offer this guidance: **be more committed to the connection with your woman than to avoiding your fears and her intensity**. When the hurt, anger, fear, and anxiety within you scream at you to pull away, **remember your deepest intention**: to stay grounded, to be connected to this woman, to be with THIS woman.

When the urge to run, defend, explain, attack, or withdraw arises, simply say to yourself *"No, I am not doing that."* Rely on all of the techniques I've given you. Use your breath. See her vulnerable side. Become present. Hear her pain rather than the blame. Ask for a pause. Use the embodiment exercises to develop your nervous system capacity. Anything. Whatever it takes to fight through your reactivity and stay true to your deeper intention.

And there will be times when she shuts you out in an effort to escape her own fear and anxiety. She may attack you, insult you, storm out of the room, or hang up on you. My guidance is to steadfastly **refuse the rejection**. Don't accept that your woman, in her chaotic and obviously impaired state, gets to unilaterally shut down the connection. YOU choose to keep the connection open.

There have been times when my woman has done this. Where she was feeling so hurt she stopped communicating or told me "*Don't call me.*" This definitely triggers my abandonment issues. I hate it, but I know that deep down, it is really a test of my devotion. Her most dysfunctional part is trying to hide and isolate. But her deepest self is hoping that I will be her rock. That I will stand strong for the relationship even when she can't. That I will be there for her, despite her bad behavior. And that I will not accept her isolating herself.

So, when she tries to do this, I back off on the issue at hand and give her a little space to settle, but I stay engaged. I don't let her unilaterally shut down the connection. And I don't withdraw as a result of *her* withdrawal. I might send a simple text letting her know that I'm here for her, but without pressing too hard to be in contact or to keep hashing out the issue at hand. In that text, I could also add some structure by saying "*Let's get a good night's sleep and we can talk tomorrow*" rather than just leaving things open-ended regarding future communication.

Remember, gentlemen, this is a test. So refuse the rejection.

• • •

The fourth piece of advice I will give is to **show your love, don't just tell**. I mentioned this earlier but I would like to say more. The Feminine deeply desires to feel loved. Your verbal expressions of *"I love you"* are nice, but they only go so far. Your woman is paying more attention to what you DO than what you SAY. In other words, does your professed love translate into action?

Verbal expressions of love don't take any forethought, planning, or effort. They are just words describing a feeling in the moment. But the Feminine cannot trust it as reality or as an assurance that you'll be there for her through thick and thin. The Feminine needs to see love demonstrated in action.

Examples of things which communicate love through action include:

- Remembering your anniversary and planning an amazing date
- Picking up the milk on the way home from work when she asks
- Checking in with her periodically about something that's been troubling her, such as a challenging work or family situation
- Doing things for her that may be difficult or unpleasant for her to do herself, such as fixing the garage door that has been sticking lately or helping her with a project which she finds challenging

Some of these may seem mundane, or to have nothing to do with how much you love her. But to her, they absolutely are proxies for love. Because **to love her is to keep her and her needs in your field of attention**. When you fail to do some of these things, particularly if you forget, it is painful for her because it feels forgotten by you. That she's not top of mind for you.

The Feminine expects the Masculine to be action-oriented. So she feels let down without these action-oriented Masculine expressions of love. Remember this the next time she's upset with you for forgetting to pick up milk and you're wondering "*What's the big deal?*" **You think it's about the milk, but to her it is about love.**

In fact, "acts of service" is one of the five love languages identified by Gary Chapman: words of affirmation, acts of service, receiving gifts, quality time, and physical touch. I encourage you to read about this framework. Each of us has one or two primary love languages. For your woman to feel your love, it needs to be conveyed in one of her primary languages. And despite your best intentions, love conveyed through a non-primary language doesn't impact her nearly as much.

I know a lot about this because my woman's primary love languages are touch and acts of service. Thankfully, touch is one of my primaries, so we connect well there. But acts of service are not a primary for me, so it is not my organic orientation. But this is what *she* needs to feel loved. I can tell her I love her ("words of affirmation"), but it only lands with about fifty percent effectiveness. To feel fully loved, she needs me to DO things that SHOW my care for her. Since this doesn't come naturally to me, if I want my woman to feel deeply loved, then I have to make the effort to express in HER language.

So, if your woman has acts of service as a primary love language, as many do, then you need to SHOW her how much you love her, not just TELL her.

• • •

Fifth, **you will never get credit for your past good deeds with your woman.** This principle is from David Deida, who writes that all of the reliability, love, and trustability that you've demonstrated through the years with your woman goes right out the window when she's upset. The Feminine lives in the moment. All it knows is what it feels right now. If, after years of loving and leading your woman with a lot of skill, you drop the ball on something, expect that sometimes she will react as if nothing of that track record ever existed. In her emotional state, she CANNOT remember the past.

As a man, you'll be thinking to yourself *"Sheesh, after all I've done for her over the years, why is she getting so mad and not trusting me? She knows I love her and knows that I lead her well!"* You'll be quoting to her a laundry list of things you've done well. Yet to the Feminine, in the moment, it all means nothing. Resting on your laurels or coasting are not possible with your woman. I encourage you to internalize this lesson immediately and save yourself a lot of false hope.

To be honest, I still struggle with accepting this one. My reactive side thinks it's crazy. But my deeper knowing recognizes it as a fundamental reality.

• • •

Our sixth principle is that you should **know that you can usually ask for a do-over**. Sometimes you'll just be plain clumsy in dealing with your woman. You might say something careless and hurt her feelings. You might make a bad assumption. Or she might just misunderstand what you said or meant. Suddenly, you find yourself in a fight you never intended to have. A do-over can be an easy way out. If the context of the fight is not a "code red" issue and it hasn't progressed too far, you can simply pause and ask for the do-over: *"Baby, can we have a do-over? I messed up and I now realize it. I'd like to try that again in a way that is more in line with my intention."*

I find this to be one of the more elegant ways to pull out of meaning-less and unintended conflict. Use it. She WILL notice your skill and appreciate your leadership.

• • •

The seventh principle is one of the most effective things you can do in dealing with your woman: **accept her as your Feminine "Oracle"**. I've mentioned this concept of an Oracle in a prior chapter. It is the acknowledgment that your woman has a Feminine intuition that you do not possess. That she can reflect things back to you of which you would otherwise not be aware. She may do it skillfully or toxically, but in either case, it is information for you to consider.

In practice, when your woman is complaining, challenging you, or giving you a reflection which is difficult to take, you should try to not immediately disagree or get defensive. If you accept her as your Oracle, you will, for the moment, give her the benefit of the doubt and consid-er what she might be showing you. If she's doing it toxically, you might need to bring her back to her heart, to get her to "share her pain" more cleanly. Or you might have to look underneath her complaint to find that pain (which means doing a little translation yourself if she can't). But you stay open to what she has to share.

This does not mean that she's always right, or that you discard all of your own instincts. It simply means that you temporarily pause your resistance, trust her instincts, and make space to consider what they show you.

In my own relationships, my Achilles' heel had traditionally been my defensiveness. So adopting this simple practice created a huge shift for both my partner and me. Instead of having my ego invested in my own perspective, I simply decided to start trusting my woman's intuition, which I already knew to be highly developed but I wasn't always listening to in practice.

CONCLUSION

Successfully dealing with your woman when she's fired up can be one of the more difficult things you do in life. But remember one thing: her chaotic emotions are the flipside of the Feminine juiciness that you enjoy. You can't have one without the other. If you can love and lead her well, that Feminine energy will be channeled into the juice rather than the toxicity.

David Deida often says: don't ever expect your woman to change or get easier. I disagree with the absoluteness of the statement. She *will* change, but not of her own volition. Her behavior will change when you change When you start living from your Masculine core and leading the relationship. The more consistent and skillful you are, the more her storms will start to abate.

CHAPTER 15

HEART

Your woman wants to feel you in your heart. It makes her feel safer, and therefore more open. She wants to feel you in your heart just like she wants you in your power. She needs this in order to open to your lead.

And you probably have no idea what that means.

Don't worry — most men don't. I will try to shed some light on the topic in this chapter.

MEN AVOID THEIR HEART

The Feminine is wired to crave love and connection. This is biological in nature. Your woman probably withers without these two elements. The Feminine manifests love and needs to see it reciprocated by her partner. She needs to FEEL your capacity to love and experience emotion.

Remember that in relationship, you are not just two islands of "Me". The two of you are a "We". You are the other half of the emotional equation to her. When you're not in your heart, she feels pain in hers.

This doesn't mean that you are codependent, but rather that your emotional states impact her.

Unfortunately, most men manifest their love through cognitive expression and by being a Provider for their beloved and/or family. So you get confused when your woman expresses a lack in this domain. You might say to her (or just yourself): *"What do you mean I'm not in my heart? I tell you that I love you all the time! And I work incredibly hard to take care of you."* But the Feminine needs to feel your open heart in order to feel truly loved.

Being in your heart is far more than saying *"I love you"* and working your ass off to support her. It is the capacity to feel your emotions, and to feel hers. It is the ability to come out of your thinking mind and into your feeling body. Instead of logic and evaluation, you're offering empathy. Empathy is the ability to truly feel what another person is feeling. It is not just a knowing of the mind, but rather a felt experience.

And, it is the ability to share what's inside, speaking to the deeper emotions within you rather than just the anger, stories, and blame on top.

Unfortunately, **most men are terrible at this,** for a very simple reason: we try to avoid emotional pain at all costs.

Your heart is the epicenter of where you feel your emotions. All of your negative emotions — anger, fear, shame, sadness — occur as PAIN in the heart. **Men do NOT want to feel this kind of pain**. So, you assiduously avoid it. You close your heart and exist in the world via your mind. You roll through life with logic and goal orientation so that you don't have to feel the emotional pain.

The pain you avoid is analogous to the old boxes in your garage that you've procrastinated dealing with for years. It's too much trouble to spend the time unpacking them and figuring out what to do with the contents. So you opt to just step around them, year after year.

This is what men do. Instead of opening to the pain and feeling it fully, you suppress and avoid it. You claim that you don't feel anything (despite your woman clearly sensing otherwise). You're pragmatic and logical. You live with a "get it done" attitude, with no time for pointless emotions to bog you down. You deflect it through humor. You change the subject. You focus on facts. You maintain an *"everything's fine"* facade.

To you, emotional pain is a burden and a distraction.

For most men, this habit has origins in childhood. We're taught not to cry. Not to be a wuss. To suppress our feelings, be strong, and stay productive.

And yet, if you won't feel your own pain, you certainly will not feel your woman's pain. You'll try to avoid that too. And as we looked at in Chapter 14, much of the Feminine "bitchiness, nagging, and irritability" is actually just her clumsy expression of the pain of not feeling connected, loved, or led. Pain that she's dying for you to just hear.

But your closed heart won't hear it. You'll block out her pain by ignoring it, going defensive, or prematurely attempting to fix it. You will not be capable of the empathy that she's craving.

In this state, your woman won't fully trust you. She won't feel fully safe with you. She won't fully open to you. **You will never have the level**

of playfulness, respect, acceptance, and sexual openness that you desire if you don't learn to open your heart.

Say what you want about overt emotionality being the domain of the wuss. You're in relationship with a *woman*, and she sets the rules for what opens her. If she's going to surrender to you, she requires your open heart.

If you're angry at someone, your woman wants to hear you admit your anger. If you experience deep loss, your woman wants to see and feel you openly embodying your sadness. If you fear some outcome in life, she doesn't want to hear "*I'm fine*" from you, but rather wants to see you own that fear.

She does not want to hear you denying having these emotions. Nor cracking a joke to deflect and avoid. Or being needy and dumping your emotions on her, expecting her to do something to make it all better.

No, she wants to feel you present and steady as you acknowledge, own, and embody whatever emotion you feel.

My particular Achilles' heel around emotion is admitting when I'm angry at my woman. I'll deny, deflect, say I'm fine, or use humor to avoid. The small part of me thinks that's the easy way out. Yet all along, my woman is just dying for me to speak what's true within me. And, yes, heart-centeredness even includes anger.

It's so simple. Just be true about what's inside you, and feel it while you share it. And bring empathy when she's sharing what's true for her. Being in your heart is really that simple, even while it is incredibly hard for most men to do.

And lest you think that an open heart only applies to your interactions with your woman, I can tell you it applies elsewhere. It can manifest in the form of "tough love". Imagine your child or a male friend doing something that is clearly harmful to them, their interests, or someone else. You want the best for this person. So, you don't ignore or avoid the issue, nor do you impotently complain or shame them. Rather, you come at them strong, connected to a deep place of care and a desire to protect or help them. From this place, you can call them out, set a boundary, and even just express the impact on you of seeing them self-sabotage. But you don't back down or water it down. A man in his heart can do this in a powerful and grounded way.

Imagine seeing your son perform poorly in school because he is playing too many video games. Imagine learning that a friend is being unfaithful to his woman. Or watching another friend chronically ignore his woman's pleas for something different in their relationship, right up to the brink of her walking out. Dropping into your heart will enable a gravitas and groundedness when you say: "*Son/Brother — I care about you too much to let you do this to yourself ...* " The deep care for them that you let yourself feel powers your ability to set a strong boundary or challenge them to be better. This is what being in your heart enables.

HOW TO OPEN YOUR HEART

Opening your heart requires you to do something very difficult and courageous: open to the pain. Hers, yours, and the world's. It is really not that complicated. You aren't required to solve the pain. Only to open to it and feel it.

Being in your heart starts with a slowing down, a settling into the present moment. It's hard to be in your heart in the chaos of logistics and life. Slowing down and feeling is the antithesis of the "get it done" mentality in which you live most of the time. You'll need to learn to pop out of that mode. NOTHING about being in your heart exists in the past and future. It is a 100 percent "now" experience. You come out of your thinking mind while using more of your eyes, ears, and feeling body.

Heartfulness entails leaving behind any notion of right or wrong. Or of how to fix anything. You're just being with what is. It is a space of compassion, connection, and caring.

Let's look at an example. I remember a time that my woman was upset that I hadn't installed her newly purchased cell phone holder for her car before I left for a week of travel. She had been feeling that she'd taken too many risks while driving by not having one, so she was eager to get it installed. I ran out of time to do it before I left for my trip. When she called to express her disappointment, my brain-oriented response was to defend myself by explaining how we'd gotten to her place late from our hike, and we'd simply run out of time for me to install the holder before I left for the airport. Of course, you know by now where that type of fact-centered defensiveness will lead.

For me, it was an issue of not enough time. But for her, it was an issue of not enough care and protection, because she was feeling all of the fear of having to continue driving while distracted and wanted me to protect her from that. And the pain of feeling that I wasn't making her a priority. So, of course, her expression came out laced with toxicity. And of course, I got defensive.

But dropping into my heart would have offered new possibilities. In that state, my attention would naturally move away from myself and the compulsion to preserve my "goodness". This would allow me to look beyond myself and actually feel HER, and what's happening for her.

My attention would have organically shifted toward care. In that place, I would be able to feel what it's like to be in her shoes. To see her perspective through her eyes. From there, I'd have been capable of saying *"Oh Baby, of course you felt I wasn't taking care of you by making sure it got installed. You've been worried about how you have to fumble for your phone when it rings while you're driving and that feels unsafe"* instead of trying to debate facts with her and convince her that she shouldn't be upset.

We've talked a lot in previous chapters about how hearing her pain, rather than the blame, can help in situations like this. We've talked about how training your nervous system to handle intensity can help. In this chapter, I'm telling you that dropping into your heart is another powerful way of staying grounded and available in the face of emotional intensity.

But instead of doing this, we men hold on tightly to preserving our "rightness" or "goodness". We over-focus on the facts while completely missing the emotional reality right in front of us.

Now, being in your heart is not just about opening to her pain. It is also a path to expressing your own. We talked in Chapter 9 about how healthy it is to express your anger. But anger and resentment are emotions that usually cover up other emotions like fear and shame. Dropping into your heart helps you access, feel, and express these deeper emotions hidden behind the anger. You are allowing yourself to feel them, and that is the only path toward releasing their energy so they don't covertly run you.

But you will resist letting go of the tight grip that closes your heart to her feelings or your own. It is like that moment before jumping from the plane in skydiving: it's hard as hell to let go of the handrail and fall into the unknown. Emotions are messy to deal with, particularly for men. Too much trouble.

It's easier to simply not deal with them. So you claim *"I'm fine"*, make a joke, or just ignore the pain. But your short term avoidance strategy will nearly always lead to relationship problems in the long term. It's naive to think you can get away with avoiding the tough stuff. She notices it, and she remembers. Every time you dodge feeling or expressing the hard emotions it breaks trust. It's not real. It is the opposite of courage. In her eyes, it is what a coward does.

This is the moment of choice you must master. When the world or your woman trigger you, make the choice that the way out will not be through holding on tighter, but by simply letting go and sinking into your heart without defense.

Practice by yourself at first and learn to get past your resistance. For me, the best way to induce myself into a heartful state is to think of my children. I notice myself soften and open, and my care and regard move from my own selfish needs to their well being. I am capable of feeling their pain in the moment, sometimes even more than they do. Practice this yourself so that you get to know the feeling. If you don't have children, then think of any being in your life for whom your care is deep — a sibling, a grandmother, or even a pet. You'll likely notice that heartfulness comes naturally to you with this visualization.

As you do this, notice that going into your own pain won't hurt you. All the resistance you've previously felt is just a mirage fooling you into playing it safe. You need only surrender to the feelings and let them rewire your nervous system with a knowing that you'll be OK.

Now, in this state, bring your woman into your mind's eye. Imagine her feeling deep sadness over something. Overlay the softness and empathy from the prior visualization onto her. Offer it as a gift to her in your mind's eye. Her deepest Feminine craving is to be heard, seen, and felt. In this softer, heart-centered place, this will come much more easily to you.

Now, imagine her upset with *you*, and maintain this empathy. Stay present to hearing her pain, even if she's blaming you for causing it. Just feel what it's like to be in her emotional shoes.

The embodiment practices we discussed before can be helpful in this regard. It is much easier to go into your heart when you're already in your body. If you're in your head, then the mind will have much more control over you. It will hold on tightly and scream at you that you absolutely do NOT want to feel your heart. It is a powerful siren song which few men can resist. But if you can combine an embodiment practice, hearing of her pain, and the steps I suggested above, you'll be well prepared to go toward the pain rather than run away from it.

WHY BE IN YOUR HEART?

Men almost always ask why they should try to be in their heart. Is it because they are "supposed" to do so, out of some obligation to be a "nice guy"? No. Absolutely not. Being heartful does not necessarily mean being nice, as we saw in my earlier comments about tough love. But it is about tuning in to what's real.

In fact, there are some great selfish reasons why it is in your best interest to develop this capacity.

Women will tell you there is a feeling of availability around a man in his heart. Being vulnerable and sharing your pain makes you more attractive to her because she'll feel closer to you. This is in contrast to when you're a stone that has it all together — inaccessible to her and seemingly unimpacted by her. The less you hide, the more you seem comfortable in your own skin.

Women will also tell you they feel safer around such a man because they can show their pain and know it will be received with empathy rather than dropped, ignored, or defended against.

The more you do this, the more she trusts you. The more devoted to you she will become, barring other factors. And if you are reading this book, you're desiring a woman who is devoted and adoring rather than irritable, critical, and sexually closed.

With your heart open, you'll hear and be present for her pain. And you will be shocked — yes, shocked — at how quickly this diffuses her intense emotions. Honestly, it is like magic. Yet somehow men sometimes choose to go the path of avoidance or defensiveness — author included. Let your open heart be your secret weapon in your quest to lead you and your woman to a better place relationally. I can say from personal experience that I am almost always more successful with my woman when I manifest heartfulness rather than cognition.

The other benefit to being in your heart is that it actually **makes her anger seems a little less intense.** Because when you're in your heart and feeling empathy, you're **naturally** hearing the PAIN louder than the BLAME (as we discussed in Chapter 14). It just organically shifts your perceptions. So when she's raging at you, it will seem a little softer and easier to be with. She won't seem so scary. Her anger won't be so threatening. You'll be more grounded and present without even trying.

I'll share a principle that I learned from Leonard Jacobson: it is more effective to BE love rather than try to GET love from your partner. So when she's angry with you, being in your heart makes this much more possible. Instead of being reactive to her anger, you'll be in a heartful place, able to exude the love that she temporarily cannot. When she experiences this way of being in you, it nearly always has the effect of softening her.

Doing this creates a virtuous cycle. It calms her down in this moment, and lays the groundwork for her to trust you more next time.

Remember that her anger is almost always her expression of pain due to a break in connection between the two of you. **She seems like she wants to destroy you, but ironically she just wants to feel closer to you.** Being in your heart helps you see it as such.

Many women talk about wanting a man with depth. A big part of depth is this capacity to feel all of life's realities — pain, joy, sadness, suffering, loss, and hope. It is like catnip for the Feminine. It draws women in. To them, a man's capacity for heart and depth translates into a deep personal power and wisdom. Most women crave such qualities in their man. They're hungry for it.

Please know that being a warrior and being in your heart are NOT mutually exclusive. To be in your heart does not suggest you are a poetry-reading wimp. And yes, I'm being tongue in cheek there with the poetry comment, but only to combat common male misconceptions and defenses around heart-centeredness.

CONCLUSION

Being heartful isn't fluff. It is simply a choice to feel your own heart, and feel into your woman's pain when she's upset. This is not a natural act for most men, but with practice you can learn to cultivate this capacity for love and heartfulness. When you do this, she will experience your depth and a profound sense of emotional safety.

CONCLUSION

Congratulations on getting this far. You've taken a long journey of exploring the dynamics of Polarity, and how you can harness them to improve your relationship. In parting, I will share a few words of wisdom.

First, don't feel the need to tell your woman about the work you're doing. Just live it. Talking about it too much carries the scent of trying too hard to get a gold star from her. Do this for YOU.

Second, don't do this alone. You need the company of other men on this journey. We're all in this together, and we often have similar challenges. Join a men's group, or see my website for more information on *The MIR Community*.

Third, don't stop with just reading a book. It's not enough to create lasting change. See gsyoungblood.com for the *Art of Relational Masculinity*™ online course and live workshop. Both will help you deepen your absorption of the work.

Fourth, start a daily embodiment practice. You can't do this with just cognitive knowledge. You must work on grounding the nervous system. See my website for the *Art of Embodiment* book and online course.

Keep up the good work. Your woman and your family need you to do this. The world needs you to do this.

APPENDICES

THE ART OF RELATIONAL MASCULINITY™ ONLINE COURSE

If you enjoyed this book and want to go deeper, then *The Art of Relational Masculinity* online course is for you. Based on the same three part *Masculine Blueprint,* it contains my newest principles and practices that will help you further build your *Masculine Core.*

- First, we'll dive deep into **Respond vs. React.** I give a short primer on embodiment and demonstrate a few practices you can use right away. I also offer three very counterintuitive ways to curb your own reactivity, as well as help you deal with what feels like "crazy".
- Second, we explore **Provide Structure.** I start by presenting my *Directional Energy Framework.* We then delve deep into how you can bring more leadership into each of the three primary domains of your life: Logistical, Emotional, and Sexual.
- Finally, we'll discuss **Create Safety.** I teach you how to create deep emotional connection with your woman, such that criticism and fights wane, while nurturing, ease, and sexuality start to thrive in your relationship.

These are my newest and most powerful teachings. If you're done tolerating a mediocre or toxic relationship, this course is your path to a new reality.

Purchase at gsyoungblood.com/arm

THE ART OF EMBODIMENT
ONLINE COURSE

If the discussion in Chapter 10 on embodiment appealed to you, then go deeper with *The Art of Embodiment for Men* book and online companion course.

The handbook is available on Amazon, and teaches you how to build your own regular embodiment practice.

And the online video course takes it even further. You'll get:

- Additional insights, over and above the book, on the principles and practices
- Visual demonstrations of some of the physical practices
- Additional practices, including "embodied voice", the *Cold Immersion Protocol* and *Candle Practice*
- Over 35 audio guided sessions to help you learn the practices and keep a consistent daily routine

Sign up at gsyoungblood.com/aoe

Printed in Great Britain
by Amazon

29978612R00173